The Ultimate Gaming Laptop Buying Guide

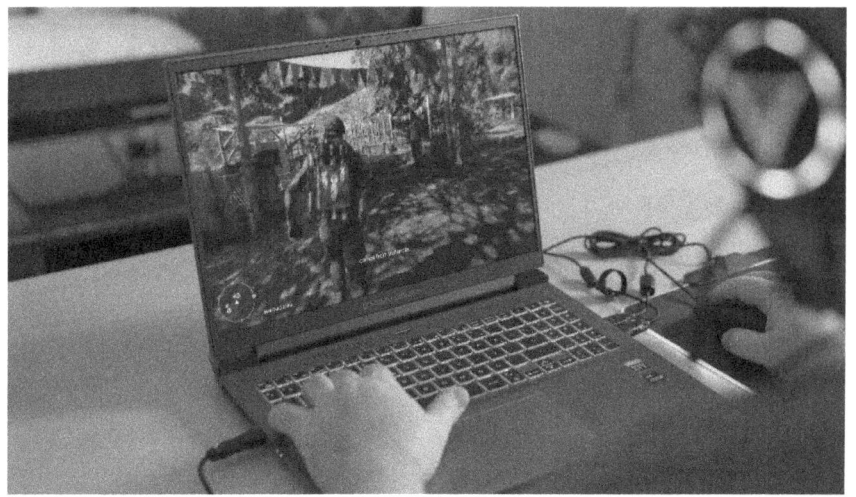

Essential Reviews and Performance Insights to Help Beginners Choose the Ideal Gaming System

Robert I. Grass

Copyright © 2024 Robert I. Grass

All rights reserved. No part of this book may be reproduced, stored in a retrieval system, or transmitted in any form or by any means—electronic, mechanical, photocopying, recording, or otherwise—without the prior written permission of the publisher, except in the case of brief quotations used in reviews or critical articles.

Disclaimer

This Gaming Laptop Buying Guide is for informational purposes only. While every effort has been made to ensure accuracy, the author and publisher are not responsible for errors, omissions, or changes in product specifications, pricing, or availability.

Readers are encouraged to conduct their own research and consult with professionals or retailers when making a purchase. Brand names and trademarks mentioned are the property of their respective owners and are included for identification purposes only.

Decisions made using the information in this guide are the sole responsibility of the reader.

Table of Contents

Introduction 9

    Understanding the Evolving Gaming Laptop Market 13

    How This Guide Will Help You Make the Right Choice 15

Chapter 1: Understanding Gaming Laptops 18

    What Makes a Laptop "Gaming"? 18

    Key Differences Between Gaming and Regular Laptops 22

    How Gaming Laptops Have Evolved 27

    From Heavy Beasts to Sleek Powerhouses 30

    The Rise of Thin-and-Light Gaming Laptops 31

    What to Expect from a Gaming Laptop: Performance vs. Price 34

Chapter 2: Key Features To Look For In A Gaming Laptop 41

    The Processor (CPU): The Brain Behind Your Laptop 42

The Graphics Card (GPU): Powering Your Visuals 47

RAM (Memory): Why It's Crucial for Gaming Performance 56

Storage: SSD vs. HDD – What's Best for Gamers? 60

Display Quality: Getting the Best Visuals 66

Keyboard & Build Quality: Comfort and Durability for Long Sessions 77

Cooling Systems and Ventilation: Keeping Your Laptop Cool 79

Build Materials: Plastic vs. Aluminum 83

Battery Life: How to Balance Power with Portability 86

Chapter 3: Gaming Laptops for Every Budget 91

Budget Gaming Laptops (Under $800) 92

Top Budget Models and What They Offer 95

Mid-Range Gaming Laptops ($800 - $1500) 97

Recommended Mid-Range Models ($800 - $1500) 103

High-End Gaming Laptops ($1500 and Above) 108

Premium Models That Offer Cutting-Edge Performance 112

Chapter 4: Choosing a Gaming Laptop Based on Your Gaming Style 115

Casual Gamers: Finding a Laptop for Casual Gaming and Entertainment 116

Competitive/Esports Gamers: Laptops for High-Speed, Professional Gaming 122

Content Creators and Streamers: Gaming Laptops for Multi-Tasking and Streaming 126

VR Gamers: Laptops for Virtual Reality Gaming 136

Chapter 5: How to Compare Gaming Laptops 143

Benchmarking Performance: Understanding Game Benchmarks and Reviews 144

Real-World Performance: What to Expect When Gaming 149

Frame Rate vs. Graphics Settings 153

Long-Term Considerations: Will Your Laptop Last for Future Games?... 159

Chapter 6: Additional Features and Considerations.. 165

Port Selection: Ensuring Your Laptop Has All the Right Ports.. 166

Cooling Solutions: Why Laptop Cooling is Crucial 173

Upgradability: Can You Upgrade Your Gaming Laptop?... 178

Operating System: Windows vs. Linux for Gaming 183

Which OS Should You Choose for Gaming?..... 188

Chapter 7: Troubleshooting and Maintaining Your Gaming Laptop............................... 190

Common Issues in Gaming Laptops and How to Fix Them 191

How to Maintain Your Laptop's Performance Over Time 198

When to Repair vs. Replace Your Laptop......... 207

Chapter 8: Gaming Laptop Accessories.... 212

Essential Accessories for Your Gaming Laptop Setup... 213

External Monitors, Mousepads, and Laptop Stands... 218

Peripheral Compatibility: Making Sure Everything Works Together... 221

Chapter 9: Top Gaming Laptop Models in 2024...225

Top Budget Picks..225

Top Premium Picks 236

VR-Ready and Esports Laptops 241

Chapter 10: Future Trends in Gaming Laptops (Detailed Version) 247

What's Next for Gaming Laptop Technology? .248

The Future of Gaming Laptop Design...............253

Conclusion 259

Appendix..267

Introduction

In the past few years, gaming laptops have changed a lot. They used to be big and weak, but now they're thin and powerful, on par with desktop gaming PCs.

There are so many choices and technical specs for gaming laptops that it can be hard to decide which one to buy. This guide's job is to help you find your way around this complicated world by giving you the reviews and performance information you need to make an informed choice.

That a gaming laptop is not the same as a normal laptop

At first view, a gaming laptop might look like any other laptop on the market. However, there are some important differences that make it unique.

A regular laptop usually puts portability, battery life, and general productivity features at the top of its list of priorities. This makes them great for work, reading, and casual use. Gaming laptops, on the other hand, are made to handle the heavy processing and graphics needs of current video games.

A gaming laptop is different in the following ways:

1. Power for graphics processing: Gaming laptops have powerful graphics cards (GPUs), which are needed to make the graphics in current games look real. While regular laptops usually have integrated graphics suited for everyday work, gaming laptops feature dedicated GPUs like NVIDIA

GeForce or AMD Radeon, allowing for smooth gameplay even at higher resolutions and settings.

2. Faster Processors: Gaming laptops come with more powerful CPUs that can handle the heavy lifting of running complex games, multi-tasking, and keeping high frame rates. These processors are usually Intel Core i7 or i9, or AMD Ryzen 7 and Ryzen 9, compared to the more modest chips in regular laptops.

3. Enhanced Cooling Systems: Due to the high-power output needed for gaming, these laptops are built with advanced cooling mechanisms to prevent overheating. Regular laptops often have minimal cooling, which may not be enough for extended heavy use, but gaming laptops feature larger fans, heat pipes, and sometimes even vapor chambers to keep temperatures in check.

4. Superior Displays: Gaming laptops typically boast higher refresh rates (120Hz, 144Hz, or even

240Hz), which turns into smoother visuals during fast-paced gameplay. Regular laptops often come with standard 60Hz displays that are fine for daily tasks but may leave gamers frustrated by screen tearing or lag during gaming.

5. *Customizable Features:* Many gaming laptops offer customizable RGB lighting, extra ports, and additional storage choices, catering to the personalization that gamers enjoy. This level of flexibility isn't usually a priority in regular laptops, where you'll find more uniform, simpler designs.

In summary, gaming laptops offer the kind of power and performance needed for a smooth gaming experience, whereas regular laptops are geared more toward general use, making them less suitable for handling the demands of gaming.

Understanding the Evolving Gaming Laptop Market

The gaming laptop market has seen substantial growth and diversity over the past decade. What was once a niche product for hardcore gamers is now a mainstream category with products tailored to all types of gamers, from casual players to expert eSports athletes.

1. *Technological Advancements:* As game technology has advanced, so too have the capabilities of gaming laptops. The integration of powerful graphics cards, faster processors, and high-resolution screens has improved greatly. Meanwhile, innovations in battery technology, cooling systems, and lightweight designs are pushing gaming computers to be more portable without compromising on performance.

2. *Increase in Game Complexity:* As video games become more immersive with realistic graphics and bigger worlds, the hardware requirements for gaming laptops have also increased. This has led to an expanded market with choices at various price points, from entry-level machines to premium devices with cutting-edge specs.

3. *Price Range and Options*: The rise of gaming laptops has also led in a wide range of prices and configurations. Whether you're looking for a cheap entry-level gaming laptop or a high-end system for VR or 4K gaming, there's now a machine for nearly every budget. The competition between brands has driven companies to offer more bang for your buck, especially when it comes to processing speed, graphics, and cooling.

4. *Portability and Design:* Another key shift is the focus on portability. Early gaming computers were often large, heavy, and cumbersome. Today, many manufacturers are making sleek, lightweight models without sacrificing performance. This has made gaming laptops more appealing to a wider audience who value mobility but still want a high-quality gaming experience.

The gaming laptop market is constantly evolving with technological advancements, changing gaming needs, and a wider variety of options available. This dynamic landscape can make selecting the right laptop daunting, but with the right knowledge, you can find the perfect fit for your gaming needs.

How This Guide Will Help You Make the Right Choice

With so many choices available, choosing the right gaming laptop can feel overwhelming, especially if you're new to the world of gaming. This guide is here to simplify the process, breaking down complex technical terms and helping you understand the most important features to consider when making your buy.

1. Comprehensive Reviews: We'll provide thorough reviews of popular gaming laptops, helping you compare their performance, design, and features. This will give you a clearer picture of which models are best fit for different gaming needs and budgets.

2. Performance Insights: You'll learn how to evaluate the key performance metrics of a gaming laptop, including GPU, CPU, RAM, and storage, so you can assess how each device works in terms of gaming capabilities.

3. Buyer's Tips and Considerations: The guide will also offer practical advice on factors such as price-to-performance ratio, warranty options, and long-term reliability, ensuring that you make a purchase that delivers both value and satisfaction.

Whether you're looking for an affordable option for casual gaming or a high-performance machine for professional gaming, this guide will help you understand what to look for and make a confident, informed choice.

Chapter 1: Understanding Gaming Laptops

Gaming laptops are a unique breed of computers, built with powerful hardware and performance features that cater to the high demands of modern video games. But what exactly sets them apart from regular laptops, and how have they changed to meet the growing needs of gamers? In this chapter, we'll explore the defining characteristics of gaming computers, debunk common misconceptions, and take a closer look at how these devices have advanced over the years.

What Makes a Laptop "Gaming"?

At the core of a gaming laptop is its ability to handle demanding games without compromising efficiency. But what exactly makes a laptop "gaming"? The term goes beyond just the ability to play video games—gaming laptops are optimized to provide smooth, high-performance gameplay while also handling intensive jobs like video editing, streaming, and multi-tasking. Let's break it down.

1. High-Performance GPU (Graphics Processing Unit):

The GPU is the heart of any game laptop. A gaming laptop usually comes with a dedicated graphics card, such as the NVIDIA GeForce or AMD Radeon series, which are capable of delivering the high frame rates and smooth visuals needed for modern games. In comparison, regular laptops often come with integrated graphics, which are sufficient for basic tasks but cannot handle graphically demanding games.

2. Powerful CPU (Central Processing Unit):

Gaming laptops are built with faster and more powerful CPUs that allow them to process complex game logic and handle large amounts of data without lag. While regular laptops may come with entry-level processors like Intel Core i3 or i5, gaming laptops often feature high-performance chips like Intel Core i7 or i9 or AMD Ryzen 7 and 9, which are important for running games smoothly.

3. Fast Refresh Rate Displays:

A gaming laptop usually has a display that supports higher refresh rates (e.g., 120Hz, 144Hz, or 240Hz). This is crucial for smooth gaming experiences, especially in fast-paced titles like first-person shooters (FPS) or racing games. Regular laptops usually have standard 60Hz displays, which may cause visual tearing or lag during fast-moving scenes.

4. Enhanced Cooling Systems:

Gaming laptops tend to create a lot of heat due to their powerful components. To avoid overheating and keep optimal performance, gaming laptops come with advanced cooling systems, including larger fans, heat pipes, and sometimes even vapor chambers. Regular computers, on the other hand, have basic cooling systems that can struggle under prolonged heavy use.

5. Memory and Storage:

Gaming laptops usually come with more RAM (typically 16GB or more) to handle multiple processes and apps running simultaneously, which is essential for gaming and multitasking. Storage is also a key factor; game laptops often feature high-speed solid-state drives (SSDs) that ensure fast load times, whereas regular laptops may only have traditional hard drives (HDDs), which are slower and more prone to failure.

In essence, gaming laptops are purpose-built machines designed to meet the high standards needed for modern gaming, with top-tier graphics, faster processors, and advanced cooling. These features make them significantly more powerful than regular laptops, which are tailored to casual use and office chores.

Key Differences Between Gaming and Regular Laptops

It's easy to think of a game laptop as just a regular laptop with a cool design and flashy lights. However, the differences between gaming laptops and regular laptops are substantial and stretch far beyond aesthetics.

Here's a comparison of the two:

Feature	Gaming Laptop	Regular Laptop
GPU	Dedicated, high-performance (e.g., NVIDIA GeForce or AMD Radeon)	Integrated graphics (Intel UHD, AMD Vega)
CPU	High-performance processors (Intel	Mid-range or entry-level processors (Intel

Feature	Gaming Laptop	Regular Laptop
	i7/i9, AMD Ryzen 7/9)	i3/i5, AMD Ryzen 3/5)
Display	High refresh rate (120Hz, 144Hz, or higher)	Standard refresh rate (60Hz)
Cooling	Advanced cooling systems (multiple fans, heat pipes, vapor chambers)	Basic cooling systems (single fan or none)
Memory (RAM)	16GB or more	4GB–8GB
Storage	SSD or NVMe drive (fast load times)	HDD or basic SSD
Build Design	Often bulkier, more rugged build for cooling and performance	Slim and lightweight for portability

Feature	Gaming Laptop	Regular Laptop
Price	Higher due to premium components and features	More affordable, geared toward basic use

As you can see, the key differences revolve around the components designed to boost performance in gaming laptops, especially the GPU, CPU, cooling systems, and display. Regular laptops, while excellent for work, study, and pleasure, are simply not built to handle the demands of high-end gaming. Common Misconceptions About Gaming Laptops There are several myths and misunderstandings about gaming laptops that can confuse potential buyers. Let's clear up some of the most popular ones:

1. Gaming Laptops Are Too Expensive:

While it's true that high-performance gaming laptops can be expensive, the price range is quite wide. You can find entry-level gaming laptops starting at around $600 to $700, which are capable of running many famous games at medium settings. High-end models with premium GPUs and faster CPUs can pass $2000, but there's something for every budget.

2. Gaming Laptops Are Bulky and Heavy:

In the past, gaming laptops were indeed bulky and heavy due to their strong components. However, improvements in laptop design and cooling technology have led to thinner, lighter models without compromising performance. Many current gaming laptops are sleek and portable, weighing as little as 4 to 5 pounds.

3. All Gaming Laptops Have the Same Specs:

Not all gaming laptops are made equal. There is a wide variety of specifications, from budget-friendly choices with mid-range processors and GPUs to high-end machines with the latest Intel i9 or AMD Ryzen 9 processors and NVIDIA RTX 30-series graphics. It's important to match the laptop's specs to the type of gaming you plan to do.

4. You Don't Need a Gaming Laptop for Casual Gamers:

Some people think that gaming laptops are only for hardcore gamers. In fact, gaming laptops offer a level of performance and versatility that can help casual gamers as well. With the ability to handle not just games but also video editing, content creation, and productivity tasks, a gaming laptop can be a great all-in-one option.

5. Gaming Laptops Have Poor Battery Life:

While gaming laptops generally had poor battery life due to their power-hungry components, newer models have improved in this area. Many gaming laptops today offer battery life of 6-8 hours for everyday work, though heavy gaming sessions will drain the battery faster. If you plan on gaming unplugged for long periods, it's important to consider a model with an optimal battery.

How Gaming Laptops Have Evolved

Over the years, gaming laptops have experienced a major transformation in terms of performance, design, and technology. Here are some key ways in which gaming computers have evolved:

1. Smaller, More Portable Designs:

Early gaming laptops were known for their big size and weight, often needing a backpack just to carry them. Today, however, manufacturers have managed in developing powerful gaming laptops that are thinner and more portable, without sacrificing speed. Companies like Razer, ASUS, and MSI have built ultra-thin gaming laptops that are sleek and lightweight while still packing a punch in terms of gaming capabilities.

2. Improved Cooling Systems:

One of the biggest problems for gaming laptops is managing heat. With powerful components generating a lot of heat, older models were notorious for overheating or making excessive noise. Modern gaming laptops now feature sophisticated cooling systems, such as vapor chamber cooling and liquid metal thermal paste, that allow them to run at peak speed without excessive noise or temperature spikes.

3. Enhanced Display Technologies:

In addition to having higher refresh rates (120Hz and above), many gaming laptops now feature advanced display technologies, such as OLED and IPS panels. These displays provide better color accuracy, deeper blacks, and wider viewing angles, ensuring that players get the most visually immersive experience possible. Some high-end models now even offer 4K resolution displays, great for gaming in ultra-realistic graphics.

4. Customization and Personalization:

Gaming laptops are increasingly customizable, allowing users to customize everything from RGB lighting to external accessories. Gaming laptops now often feature customizable RGB keyboards, allowing gamers to choose colors and effects based on their tastes. This personalization has become a key selling point for game enthusiasts who value aesthetics as much as performance.

5. Better Battery Life and Power Efficiency:

While gaming laptops are still not known for their battery longevity, improvements in power efficiency have allowed manufacturers to extend battery life. Newer laptops with more efficient processors and GPUs, combined with optimized software, are capable of providing better performance while using less power. As a result, gaming laptops can now provide hours of battery life for less intensive jobs. Gaming laptops have evolved from bulky, underperforming machines into sleek, high-performance devices that offer an ideal gaming experience without the need for a desktop setup. With constant advancements in technology, these laptops are only getting more powerful, portable, and versatile.

From Heavy Beasts to Sleek Powerhouses

For years, gaming laptops were associated with massive, bulky designs. These early models were large and heavy, often tipping the scales at over 10 pounds, and were more akin to desktop replacements than true portable devices. The size and weight were necessary to house the powerful components—high-end graphics cards, large screens, and robust cooling systems—that gaming required. But as technology advanced, so did the design theory behind gaming laptops. Manufacturers started focused not just on raw power, but on portability and aesthetics.

The Rise of Thin-and-Light Gaming Laptops

Today's gaming computers are significantly slimmer and lighter than their predecessors. Thanks to technological breakthroughs in component miniaturization, cooling solutions, and battery technology, gaming laptops are now more portable without losing performance.

Devices that once needed heavy-duty cooling systems and large form factors now incorporate compact, advanced cooling solutions, allowing them to achieve high performance in a sleek and lightweight design.

1. Powerful Performance in a Smaller Package

The main driver of this change towards thinner, lighter designs is the evolution of processors and GPUs. Early gaming laptops were constrained by the need to use larger, desktop-grade components, but today's laptops feature mobile-specific chips that keep performance while being more power-efficient and compact.

For example, NVIDIA's Max-Q series graphics cards are designed especially for thin laptops, offering impressive performance while using less power and generating less heat than their full-sized counterparts. Similarly, Intel's 10th and 11th Gen Core processors, as well as AMD's Ryzen mobile chips, provide desktop-level power with significantly lower power usage, which is key for smaller form factors.

2. Slimmed-Down Cooling Solutions

One of the biggest hurdles in making a gaming laptop thinner and lighter is the need for effective cooling. Overheating has historically been a major issue with high-performance gaming laptops, but manufacturers have improved cooling technology greatly. New cooling systems use smaller fans, heat pipes, and liquid cooling methods to dissipate heat more effectively.

These improvements mean that laptops can run demanding games without generating the excessive heat that made earlier gaming laptops so large and heavy. As a result, today's gaming laptops offer top-tier gaming speed in a form factor that is often no bigger than a regular ultra book.

3. Design Focused on Portability

In addition to the internal changes, the external design of gaming laptops has changed. Today's gaming computers are often sleeker, thinner, and more stylish than ever before. The rise of RGB lighting and customizable aesthetic choices has allowed makers to merge high-performance gaming with more attractive designs. Laptop models like the Razer Blade, ASUS ROG Zephyrus, and Alienware X series are all examples of how sleek, modern, and powerful gaming laptops can be, giving the best of both worlds for gamers who want performance without the burden of carrying a heavy, cumbersome machine.

With this evolution, gamers now have the option to choose from a wide range of laptops that mix portability with speed. Whether you want a laptop that you can easily carry in a backpack or a powerhouse that stays on your desk, there's now a gaming laptop made to fit nearly every need.

What to Expect from a Gaming Laptop: Performance vs. Price

Gaming laptops have become a lot more diverse, with options at nearly every price point. But what exactly can you expect in terms of performance based on how much you're ready to spend? Like any technology, gaming laptops offer a trade-off between price and performance, and understanding the relationship between the two is important for choosing the right laptop.

1. Entry-Level Gaming Laptops

For those on a budget, entry-level gaming laptops are available that can handle most games at lower levels. These laptops usually cost between $600 and $800 and offer an acceptable level of performance for casual gamers who are ready to compromise on graphics quality and game settings.

Key Features to Expect:

- GPU: Typically, an entry-level graphics card like the NVIDIA GTX 1650 or AMD Radeon RX 560X.
- CPU: A mid-range processor, often an Intel Core i5 or AMD Ryzen 5.
- RAM: 8GB of RAM, which is the minimum for games.
- Storage: A 256GB SSD, giving good speed for loading games and apps, although you may need an external drive for additional storage.

While these laptops won't be able to run the latest AAA games at high settings, they'll be perfectly fine for less demanding titles, such as esports games (e.g., League of Legends, Fortnite, or CS: GO), and will still give you a good gaming experience at medium settings.

2. Mid-Range Gaming Laptops

Mid-range gaming laptops, usually priced between $1,000 and $1,500, are more powerful and can handle modern games at higher settings without breaking a sweat. These laptops are great for gamers who want a good balance between price and performance.

Key Features to Expect:

- GPU: A mid-tier graphics card like the NVIDIA GTX 1660 Ti or RTX 3050, or AMD Radeon RX 5700.

- CPU: Intel Core i7 or AMD Ryzen 7 processors, giving a good mix of performance for both gaming and multitasking.
- RAM: 16GB of RAM, which is great for gaming and running other apps simultaneously.
- Storage: A 512GB SSD, allowing fast load times and ample space for several large games.

In this price range, you'll be able to run the latest AAA games at high settings, and most modern games will look great. Whether you're playing fast-paced first-person shooters or story-driven RPGs, mid-range gaming laptops strike a good balance between speed and price.

3. High-End Gaming Laptops

High-end gaming laptops, which can range from $2,000 to $3,000 or more, offer top-tier performance and are capable of running games at ultra-high settings, allowing 4K gaming, or even virtual reality (VR) gameplay. These laptops are aimed at enthusiasts or competitive gamers who expect the best performance and cutting-edge features.

Key Features to Expect:

- GPU: High-end graphics cards like the NVIDIA RTX 3070, 3080, or 4090, or AMD Radeon RX 6800M.
- CPU: High-performance processors like the Intel Core i9 or AMD Ryzen 9.
- RAM: 16GB to 32GB of RAM, providing seamless performance in multitasking scenarios.
- Storage: 1TB SSD, giving ultra-fast data transfer and ample space for large games and files.

These laptops are built for gamers who want to experience the latest games in 4K, take on VR gaming, or run multiple apps and streams at the same time without any speed degradation. Whether you're gaming, streaming, or creating video, these machines will handle everything with ease.

4. The Importance of Price-to-Performance Ratio

When shopping for a gaming laptop, it's important to find the right balance between price and performance. While it's tempting to go for the highest-end machine available, it's important to consider what your needs are. For example, if you're an esports player who only plays games like Fortnite or League of Legends, an entry-level laptop will likely serve, and you may not need to spend $2,000 or more on a high-end machine.

On the other hand, if you're a serious gamer who plays the latest AAA titles or uses the laptop for tasks like video editing or 3D rendering, investing in a high-end model might be a worthwhile choice. Ultimately, you should base your purchase on the amount of performance you need and what you're willing to spend.

As the gaming laptop market continues to evolve, there will be even more choices at different price points, making it easier for every type of gamer to find the right system. However, it's important to remember that with gaming laptops, you often get what you pay for—so carefully consider the performance requirements of your favorite games and how much you're willing to spend in your gaming experience.

Chapter 2: Key Features To Look For In A Gaming Laptop

When shopping for a gaming laptop, it's easy to get lost in the sea of technical specifications. However, understanding the key components that add to gaming performance will make the process much simpler. In this chapter, we will dive deep into two of the most important parts of a gaming laptop: the processor (CPU) and the graphics card (GPU).

These are the driving forces behind your laptop's performance, and getting the right combination is important for the ultimate gaming experience.

The Processor (CPU): The Brain Behind Your Laptop

The CPU is the heart of any computer. It handles all the calculations, commands, and processing tasks, basically determining how fast and smoothly your laptop runs. When it comes to gaming laptops, choosing the right CPU is important, as it impacts not just gaming performance but also multitasking, streaming, and overall laptop efficiency.

Choosing Between Intel vs. AMD

For years, Intel has been the go-to choice for high-performance processors, especially for gaming laptops. However, in recent years, AMD has made significant strides with their Ryzen series of processors, providing real competition to Intel in terms of performance and price.

1. Intel Processors

Intel's Core i7 and i9 series CPUs are some of the most powerful choices available for gaming laptops. These processors are well-known for their reliable performance and excellent single-core speeds, which are crucial for many gaming apps. Intel's higher-end processors, such as the Intel Core i9, are built for heavy gaming, content creation, and multitasking.

Pros:

- Strong single-core speed (important for gaming).

- Well-established, trusted name in the gaming laptop space.
- Great power control, leading to efficient battery life in many models.

Cons:

- Higher price point compared to AMD for equal performance.
- Limited customization choices compared to AMD's Ryzen chips in budget gaming laptops.

2. AMD Processors

AMD's Ryzen processors, especially the Ryzen 7 and Ryzen 9, have become increasingly popular in gaming laptops due to their exceptional multi-core speed and affordability. AMD has greatly narrowed the gap with Intel in gaming performance, and in some cases, they even surpass Intel's processors in multi-threaded tasks like video editing and streaming.

Pros:

- Excellent multi-core speed for gaming, video editing, and streaming.
- Better price-to-performance ratio in many cases.
- Ryzen 9 CPUs are known for handling heavy multitasking and demanding apps with ease.

Cons:

- Historically, AMD processors had weaker single-core performance (although this has changed dramatically with Ryzen 5000 series).
- Slightly higher power usage, which can lead to shorter battery life in some models.

How the CPU Affects Performance

The CPU is responsible for interpreting and processing instructions, which influences how quickly and efficiently games and applications run. For gaming, the CPU handles important tasks such as controlling the game world, processing orders from your inputs, and managing background processes.

1. *Single-Core Performance:* Many games, especially older ones or those that are less graphically intensive, depend more on single-core performance. This means that a CPU with strong single-core capabilities (like Intel's i7 or i9) can greatly improve performance in these games. For esports titles like League of Legends or Fortnite, single-core performance is important to achieving high frame rates.

2. *Multi-Core Performance:* Newer, more demanding games, especially those with big open-world environments (such as Red Dead Redemption 2 or Cyberpunk 2077), can benefit from multi-core performance. AMD's Ryzen processors shine in multi-core tasks, which allows them to handle these games' intense calculations and rendering tasks with ease. The more cores a CPU has, the better it can handle background processes while keeping smooth gameplay.

Choosing between Intel and AMD comes down to your cash and specific gaming needs. Intel CPUs tend to shine in games that prioritize single-core performance, while AMD's Ryzen processors offer strong performance in multi-core applications, making them a great choice for multitaskers and those who use their laptops for content creation as well.

The Graphics Card (GPU): Powering Your Visuals

The GPU is probably the most critical component of a gaming laptop. It decides how well your laptop can render high-quality graphics, manage frame rates, and provide smooth visuals during fast-paced action. The GPU essentially powers the game experience by drawing the images, textures, and special affects you see on the screen. Without a powerful GPU, even the best CPU will struggle to offer a satisfying gaming experience.

NVIDIA vs. AMD GPUs: Which is Best for Gaming?

When it comes to gaming laptops, the two main players in the GPU market are NVIDIA and AMD. Both companies offer high-quality graphics cards, but there are some important differences that may influence your choice.

1. NVIDIA GPUs

NVIDIA is generally regarded as the leader in the gaming GPU market. Their GeForce RTX line, which includes the RTX 3060, 3070, and 3080, are some of the best gaming GPUs available. NVIDIA GPUs are known for their raw power, ray tracing skills, and robust software ecosystem.

Pros:

Superior ray tracing technology, which creates realistic lighting and shadows for a more immersive gaming experience.

Deep learning super sampling (DLSS) technology, which uses artificial intelligence to upscale lower-resolution images to improve speed without sacrificing visual quality.

Great software support, including NVIDIA's GeForce Experience, which allows you to improve game settings and keep drivers up to date automatically.

Cons:

Generally, more expensive than AMD GPUs for similar performance.

Higher power usage, which can lead to increased heat generation and reduced battery life in laptops.

2. AMD GPUs

AMD's Radeon line of graphics cards have come a long way in recent years. While AMD was once considered the underdog in the GPU market, their recent releases, such as the Radeon RX 6000 series, offer strong competition to NVIDIA, especially in terms of price-to-performance ratio. AMD's GPUs are known for delivering great performance at a more affordable price, making them an attractive choice for budget-conscious gamers.

Pros:

- More affordable compared to NVIDIA, often offering better price-to-performance value.
- Strong gaming performance for the price, capable of handling current games at high settings.
- Integration with AMD's Ryzen CPUs, which can provide optimized speed when paired together.

Cons:

- Generally weaker ray tracing skills compared to NVIDIA.
- Smaller ecosystem of gaming apps and features like NVIDIA's DLSS.
- Drivers and software support are not as smooth as NVIDIA's, although this gap has been closing in recent years.

How the GPU Affects Performance

The GPU is the main factor in determining how a game looks and plays. It handles tasks such as rendering textures, creating realistic lighting, and processing the game's graphical effects, all of which add to a smooth and visually stunning gaming experience.

1. Frame Rates: Higher-end GPUs allow you to play games at higher frame rates, which is important for fast-paced games where responsiveness is key, such as first-person shooters or racing games. A higher frame rate (e.g., 144Hz or 240Hz refresh rate) means smoother visuals and reduced motion blur, which can give you an edge in competitive games.

2. Resolution and Graphics Settings: The GPU is also responsible for generating higher-quality textures and effects. If you want to play games at higher levels (1440p, 4K) or with ultra-high settings (like ultra-quality textures, anti-aliasing, and shadow effects), a powerful GPU is necessary. A lower-end GPU will struggle to keep up with these settings and might require you to lower the screen or settings for smooth gameplay.

3. Ray Tracing and DLSS: Modern GPUs, especially NVIDIA's RTX series, allow ray tracing and DLSS. Ray tracing models how light interacts with objects in a game, creating more realistic lighting and shadows. DLSS upscales lower-resolution images, boosting speed without sacrificing visual fidelity. These technologies elevate the gaming experience, making current games look stunning and run smoother.

When choosing a gaming laptop, the GPU is perhaps the most critical factor to consider if you want to enjoy high-quality visuals and smooth gameplay.

While AMD offers great value for money, NVIDIA's GPUs are often seen as the better choice for gamers who expect the best in terms of performance, especially when it comes to ray tracing and DLSS. In conclusion, both the CPU and GPU play pivotal parts in gaming laptop performance. The CPU handles jobs like running the game's logic and multitasking, while the GPU is responsible for rendering visuals and creating immersive graphics. By knowing the strengths and trade-offs between Intel vs. AMD processors, and NVIDIA vs. AMD GPUs, you can choose the right components that fit your gaming needs, budget, and desired performance level.

Understanding VR-Ready Laptops

Virtual reality (VR) gaming gives a completely immersive experience, bringing players into the heart of the game world like never before. However, not all gaming laptops are prepared to handle the intense demands of VR gaming. For a laptop to be called VR-ready, it needs to meet certain performance benchmarks to ensure smooth, lag-free gameplay. VR applications require robust GPU performance, low latency, and high processing power, so picking the right gaming laptop is important if VR gaming is part of your plans.

What Makes a Laptop VR-Ready?

The key components that make a laptop VR-ready include:

1. Powerful GPU: VR demands high frame rates, usually at least 90 frames per second (FPS) to ensure a smooth experience and avoid motion sickness. This is particularly important because VR headsets require consistent frame rates to avoid any lag, which can disrupt immersion and cause discomfort. NVIDIA's RTX 30 series or AMD's Radeon RX 6000 series are ideal picks for VR.

2. High-Performance CPU: A fast processor is important for processing the complex tasks associated with VR. Intel's i7/i9 and AMD Ryzen 7/9 processors are typically needed to handle the high workload without bottlenecking the VR experience.

3. Minimum RAM: VR gaming needs a minimum of 16GB of RAM to run smoothly. This helps the system to handle the data from both the game and the VR environment without any performance dips.

4. Low Latency: VR gaming needs extremely low latency, which refers to the delay between your actions and the system's response. A low-latency laptop ensures that the game responds in real-time to your movements, providing a more immersive and comfortable experience.

When picking a gaming laptop for VR, make sure to look for models that are specifically labeled as "VR-ready" by manufacturers. This ensures that the laptop meets the necessary requirements for a seamless VR gaming experience.

RAM (Memory): Why It's Crucial for Gaming Performance

RAM, or random-access memory, is a key component in determining the speed of any computer, and gaming laptops are no exception. RAM temporarily stores data that the CPU needs quick access to, allowing for faster working and multitasking. When you start a game, RAM holds the game's assets, such as textures and models, so that the CPU and GPU can access them quickly. The more RAM you have, the more data your laptop can handle simultaneously, which directly impacts gaming speed.

How Much RAM Do You Really Need?

The amount of RAM you need in a gaming laptop relies on the types of games you plan to play, the number of applications you run concurrently, and your overall performance expectations. Here's a breakdown of what you can expect at different RAM capacities:

1. 8GB of RAM:

This is usually considered the minimum for gaming laptops. While 8GB is suitable for most casual games and older titles, modern AAA games, especially those with large open worlds or detailed graphics, may struggle to run smoothly on 8GB. If you plan to run other apps (like web browsers, video streaming, or productivity tools) while gaming, you may experience some lag or stuttering.

- Good for: Casual gaming, esports titles (like League of Legends, Fortnite, Valorant), and less demanding games.

2. 16GB of RAM:

This is the sweet spot for most gamers, giving excellent performance in current AAA games while leaving room for multitasking. A laptop with 16GB of RAM will handle big open-world games and high-resolution textures without slowdowns, and you'll also have enough memory to stream games, run background apps, or use creative tools simultaneously.

- Good for: Most current games, VR gaming, streaming, and content creation (e.g., video editing).

3. 32GB of RAM and Beyond:

If you're into heavy multitasking, content creation, or running memory-intensive apps while gaming, 32GB of RAM can give you the power to handle it all. However, for most gamers, 32GB is excessive for gaming alone unless you're also running complicated applications like video editing software or virtual machines in the background.

- Good for: Professional-level multitasking, content creators, and gamers who need to run demanding software alongside games.

Upgrading Your RAM for Future-Proofing While gaming laptops are often equipped with a set amount of RAM, many models allow for easy upgrades, which can be a great way to future-proof your system. As games become more demanding over time, upgrading your RAM can give your laptop the ability to run newer titles more quickly. When updating your RAM, keep the following tips in mind:

1. Check Maximum Capacity: Make sure your laptop allows the amount of RAM you plan to add.

Most gaming laptops allow for up to 32GB, though some high-end models may handle 64GB or more.

2. *Dual-Channel Memory:* For the best performance, try for a dual-channel configuration, which involves two sticks of RAM. This allows for faster data transfer and better gaming performance compared to single-channel RAM setups.

Upgrading RAM is one of the most cost-effective ways to improve your gaming laptop's performance, especially for handling future games and applications.

Storage: SSD vs. HDD – What's Best for Gamers?

When it comes to gaming laptops, storage is more important than just the amount of room available for your games. The speed at which you can access game files plays a huge role in overall gaming performance, especially in load times. There are two main types of storage devices in game laptops: solid-state drives (SSD) and hard disk drives (HDD). Let's take a closer look at both.

Importance of Speed and Capacity for Load Times

1. SSDs (Solid-State Drives):

SSDs are significantly faster than standard HDDs because they have no moving parts. Instead, they use flash memory to store data, which allows for much quicker read and write speeds. The faster load times offered by an SSD can greatly reduce the time it takes for games to load and make transitions between in-game areas more seamless. An SSD also results in faster boot times for the laptop itself and quick program launches.

Pros of SSDs:

- Extremely fast load times, reducing game and boot times greatly.

- More reliable and sturdy, with no moving parts that could break down over time.
- Lower power waste, which can help improve battery life.

Cons of SSDs:

- More expensive per gigabyte compared to HDDs.
- Limited storage space for the price, meaning you might need to manage storage or invest in external storage solutions.

2. HDDs (Hard Disk Drives): HDDs are the traditional storage devices, giving large capacities at a much lower price. They use mechanical parts to store and recover data, making them slower than SSDs. While HDDs are more affordable, their slower speeds can lead to long loading times, especially when dealing with large game files or open-world games.

Pros of HDDs:

- Much cheaper per gigabyte, allowing you to store more games and files at a lower cost.
- High capacity, with some drives offering up to 2TB or more of storage, which is ideal for storing a big library of games.

Cons of HDDs:

- Slower read/write speeds, leading to longer start times and more noticeable delays.
- More prone to failure over time due to the mechanical parts inside.

How to Maximize Storage without Breaking the Bank

For gamers who want to maximize storage without spending a fortune on a large SSD, a hybrid storage option may be the answer. Many gaming laptops now offer a combination of both SSD and HDD, giving the best of both worlds: fast load times with the SSD and ample storage capacity with the HDD.

Hybrid Storage (SSHD)

A hybrid storage solution, known as an SSHD (Solid-State Hybrid Drive), blends the speed of an SSD with the capacity of an HDD. This method allows the laptop to store frequently-used files (such as the operating system and your most-played games) on the SSD for faster access, while keeping less frequently accessed files on the HDD for larger capacity.

External Storage Options

If you find that your laptop's internal storage isn't enough, external storage drives (such as external SSDs or HDDs) are an excellent way to increase your capacity. External SSDs are particularly useful for gaming, as they offer fast data transfer rates for loading games and can be easily carried with you.

Optimize Storage Management

Regardless of the storage configuration, it's important to manage your storage wisely. Keep your operating system, game files, and important apps on the SSD, while moving less critical files like videos and documents to the HDD or external drives. This will ensure that you get the best speed from your system without running out of space.

In summary, having enough storage is important, but ensuring you have fast access to your games and files is even more critical. SSDs are a must for modern gaming laptops due to their speed, and a hybrid setup or external storage solutions can offer a balanced approach to keeping your games and files organized while managing costs.

Display Quality: Getting the Best Visuals

When it comes to gaming laptops, the display is one of the most important things that can make or break your gaming experience. While performance is important, it's the visuals that bring a game to life. The screen you choose can affect everything from how bright your game looks to how smooth the action feels. In this section, we'll take a deep dive into the key factors that add to display quality, including screen size, resolution, refresh rate, and response time. We'll also study the differences between 4K and 1080p displays, and the importance of advanced display technologies like IPS and OLED.

Screen Size, Resolution, Refresh Rate, and Response Time

1. Screen Size

The size of your screen is important for immersion and comfort during long game sessions. Common gaming laptop screen sizes range from 13 to 17 inches, with 15.6 inches being the sweet spot for most players. A 15.6-inch display strikes a balance between offering enough screen real estate for gameplay without sacrificing portability. Larger screens, such as those in 17-inch models, can offer more immersive views but tend to make the laptop bulkier and less portable.

- **15.6 inches:** Ideal for most gamers, offering a large enough screen without excessive weight or size.
- **17 inches:** Offers a more immersive experience, especially for simulation games or games that benefit from bigger screens, but may compromise portability.

2. Resolution

Resolution refers to the number of pixels on the screen and decides how sharp the image is. For gaming laptops, the two most popular resolutions are 1080p (Full HD) and 4K.

- ***1080p (Full HD):*** 1080p resolution has been the standard for gaming laptops for years and offers a good balance between quality and performance. It's easier to drive high frame rates on a 1080p display, meaning you can achieve smoother games even with mid-range GPUs. Most gaming laptops, especially in the mid-price range, will offer 1080p displays.

- ***4K:*** A 4K resolution provides four times as many pixels as 1080p, resulting in a significantly sharper and more detailed picture. However, 4K displays require more powerful GPUs to keep smooth frame rates, especially in graphically intensive games. While 4K is stunning for visual fidelity, it might not be necessary for most players unless you have a high-end GPU and prefer ultra-high-definition visuals.

3. Refresh Rate

The refresh rate is the number of times per second that your screen changes with new frames. A higher refresh rate results in smoother visuals, especially in fast-paced games like first-person shooters or racing games. Common frame rates include 60Hz, 120Hz, 144Hz, and 240Hz.

- ***60Hz:*** Standard for everyday use but not ideal for gaming. It may cause motion fuzz and screen tearing during fast-paced action.
- ***120Hz and 144Hz:*** These are popular in mid- to high-end gaming laptops. They provide a major boost to smoothness and responsiveness, allowing for a more fluid gaming experience.

- ***240Hz:*** Found in high-end gaming laptops, a 240Hz refresh rate offers ultra-smooth gameplay, which is especially beneficial for competitive gaming and esports where fast reactions and frame consistency are crucial.

4. Response Time

Response time refers to how quickly each pixel on the screen can change color, changing how clear fast-moving objects are on screen. A lower response time (measured in milliseconds, MS) results in a clearer and more precise picture, reducing motion blur and ghosting.

- ***1ms to 3ms:*** Ideal for competitive gaming and esports, where clarity and fast response times are important.
- ***5ms to 7ms:*** Acceptable for most gamers, but might show slight ghosting in very fast action scenes.

A mix of a high resolution, fast refresh rate, and low response time will ensure that your gaming laptop offers clear, smooth, and responsive visuals during your gaming sessions.

4K vs. 1080p: What's the Right Choice?

When it comes to gaming laptop displays, choosing between 1080p and 4K depends on several factors, including your game preferences, the GPU you're using, and the performance you want to achieve.

1. 1080p (Full HD)

Pros:

- Easier to run at high frame rates, even with mid-range GPUs, providing smooth gameplay.
- Less demanding on the laptop's hardware, meaning you can get better total performance, especially in competitive gaming where frame rate consistency is key.

- More affordable than 4K displays, allowing you to spend more in other important components like the GPU and CPU.

Cons:

- Lower pixel density means the image isn't as sharp as 4K, though this is less obvious on smaller screens like 15.6 inches.
- Lack of ultra-high-definition visuals, which may be a downside for those who prefer amazing graphics in single-player games.

2. 4K

Pros:

- Exceptional image clarity and sharpness, especially on larger screens. Ideal for immersive, cinematic encounters.
- Better for content creation, video editing, and watching high-definition movies or VR experiences.

Cons:

- Requires a powerful GPU (like the NVIDIA RTX 30-series or AMD Radeon RX 6000-series) to keep smooth gameplay, especially at ultra settings in graphically demanding games.
- Can cause a major drop in frame rates, which may not be ideal for competitive gaming.
- Expensive and can drain battery life quickly due to the high quality.

For most gamers, 1080p is a good choice that balances performance and visual quality. However, for those wanting the sharpest visuals and are willing to invest in powerful hardware, 4K offers an unparalleled visual experience, especially for single-player games, but may not be necessary for everyone.

The Importance of IPS and OLED Displays

The quality of the monitor panel itself is just as important as resolution and refresh rate. The two most famous display panel technologies for gaming laptops are IPS (In-Plane Switching) and OLED (Organic Light Emitting Diode).

1. IPS Displays

IPS panels are known for their color accuracy, wide viewing angles, and general consistency. They offer better color reproduction and are less prone to color warping when viewed from the side. This makes IPS displays a great choice for gamers who value vibrant and true-to-life colors, such as those playing visually stunning games or engaging in content creation.

Pros of IPS:

- Excellent color precision and vibrant colors.
- Wide viewing angles, meaning the display stays consistent even when viewed from an angle.
- Great for general productivity, picture editing, and media consumption.

Cons of IPS:

- Slightly slower response times compared to TN panels (although newer IPS models have greatly improved).
- Typically, more expensive than regular TN panels, but they're a major upgrade in terms of visual quality.

2. OLED Displays

OLED screens are becoming increasingly popular in premium gaming laptops. Unlike traditional LCD panels, OLED screens do not require a backlight, as each unique pixel emits its own light. This results in deep blacks, high contrast ratios, and vivid colors.

OLED screens are also faster in terms of response time and refresh rate, making them ideal for gamers who want the best visual experience.

Pros of OLED:

- Deep, true blacks due to the power to turn off individual pixels.

- Extremely high contrast ratios, resulting in more vibrant colors and lifelike pictures.
- Excellent for movies, media viewing, and games with dark scenes.

Cons of OLED:

- Can be more expensive than IPS screens.
- Potential for burn-in (where static images leave permanent traces on the screen), although this is becoming less of a problem with newer OLED technologies.
- Lower peak brightness compared to high-end IPS screens, which might be noticeable in bright environments.

When choosing between IPS and OLED, it depends on your taste for color accuracy and black levels. IPS is great for general use, content creation, and gaming, while OLED is ideal for players who want the deepest blacks and most vibrant colors, especially if you're looking for a more cinematic experience.

Keyboard & Build Quality: Comfort and Durability for Long Sessions

Gaming computers aren't just about raw performance—they also need to be comfortable and durable, especially if you plan to play for hours on end. The keyboard is an integral part of this, as it's your main input device. The quality of your keyboard, as well as the overall build of the laptop, can greatly affect your gaming experience.

The Best Key Travel and Typing Experience

Key travel refers to the distance a key moves when you press it. A key with a longer travel distance usually feels more satisfying and provides more tactile feedback, which can improve typing speed and reduce fatigue during long sessions.

1. Key Travel: For gaming, the ideal key travel is usually around 1.5mm to 2.0mm, which allows for responsive and comfortable keystrokes. Laptops with mechanical key switches (like those found in gaming laptops from brands like Razer and Alienware) tend to provide better feedback and a more comfortable typing experience.

2. *Typing Experience:* The quality of the key switches, the layout, and the general key spacing can make a big difference. A good game keyboard should have responsive keys that are easy to press without feeling too soft or too stiff. Anti-ghosting and N-key rollover (the ability to register multiple key presses at once) are also important for gaming, especially in fast-paced games.

In terms of build quality, look for laptops that are sturdy enough to survive long hours of use and travel.

A durable chassis made of aluminum or magnesium alloy tends to be more reliable than plastic, providing both security and a premium feel. The keyboard should be backlit, giving both functionality in low-light environments and an aesthetic touch. High-quality gaming computers often feature customizable RGB lighting, giving you the ability to personalize the look of your setup.

In conclusion, when it comes to the display, keyboard, and general build quality, paying attention to the details can make a significant impact on your gaming experience. Whether it's the smoothness of your screen's refresh rate, the richness of the colors on your display, or the comfort of your keyboard during long sessions, these factors contribute to both your immersion and pleasure.

Cooling Systems and Ventilation: Keeping Your Laptop Cool

Gaming laptops are powerful machines that produce a significant amount of heat due to the high-performance components inside them. Without proper cooling, these components can overheat, leading to throttling (reduced speed), instability, or even hardware damage. That's why cooling systems and ventilation play a critical role in ensuring your gaming laptop works smoothly, even during extended gaming sessions.

Cooling Systems in Gaming Laptops

Most gaming laptops feature a combination of fans, heat pipes, and vents to control heat. High-end models might even add liquid cooling or vapor chamber cooling for more efficient heat dissipation. Here's a breakdown of the most popular cooling solutions you'll find:

1. Fans: The most common cooling option in gaming laptops is a fan, or a set of fans, that helps push heat away from the CPU, GPU, and other components. These fans work in tandem with heat pipes to pull heat away from vital components and push it out through the laptop's vents.

2. Heat Pipes: Heat pipes are thermal conductors that help move heat away from sensitive components like the CPU and GPU. These are generally paired with fans to improve cooling efficiency. They work by using the concept of evaporation and condensation to absorb and release heat.

3. Vapor Chamber Cooling: Vapor chambers are a more advanced cooling option found in high-end gaming laptops. They are basically a flat, thin structure that uses vapor to transfer heat across a larger area. This technology ensures more even heat transfer and is highly effective in cooling the laptop's internals.

4. Liquid Cooling: Some premium gaming laptops incorporate liquid cooling systems, which are meant to cool both the CPU and GPU. These systems use a liquid coolant that flows through tubes attached to the components and is cooled by external fans. While liquid cooling is highly effective, it is generally reserved for top-tier gaming laptops due to the complexity and cost of the system.

Ventilation and Airflow

Proper airflow is just as important as the cooling system itself. A well-ventilated laptop ensures that heat can be effectively released and doesn't build up inside. The placement of vents, as well as the overall airflow design, is important in determining how well a laptop will cool itself.

Gaming laptops with carefully placed exhaust vents—often at the back or sides—ensure that hot air is quickly expelled. Laptops with intake and exhaust vents positioned near the bottom or sides typically experience better airflow, which helps in keeping lower temperatures. Additionally, larger and more efficient cooling fans add to a better flow of air through the system.

Signs of Poor Cooling Systems

A good cooling system is important to ensure that your gaming laptop performs optimally during long sessions. If you notice your laptop's fans running constantly at high speeds, loud fan noise, or if the system is prone to overheating and throttling (slowing down to avoid overheating), it might suggest inadequate cooling. Always look for laptops with a reputation for effective cooling solutions, such as those from names like ASUS ROG, Alienware, and MSI, which are known for their high-quality thermal management.

Build Materials: Plastic vs. Aluminum

The materials used in the building of a gaming laptop affect not only its appearance and durability but also its cooling performance. Most gaming laptops are made of either plastic, aluminum, or a mix of both. Let's study how each material impacts the laptop's overall performance.

1. Plastic

Plastic is often used in budget-friendly gaming computers due to its affordability and flexibility. Plastic chassis are lighter and less expensive to make, making them an attractive choice for manufacturers who want to keep costs down. However, plastic is less durable than metal and can be prone to cracking or warping under pressure. Plastic builds may also retain heat more than metal ones, leading to higher temperatures during extended game sessions.

Pros:

- Affordable and lightweight.
- Easier to make into different shapes.
- More budget-friendly for entry-level gaming computers.

Cons:

- Less durable, prone to scratches and cracks.
- May not dissipate heat as quickly as metal bodies.
- Can feel cheaper or less expensive.

2. Aluminum

Aluminum is often used in higher-end game laptops for its better durability, premium feel, and ability to dissipate heat more effectively than plastic. Aluminum is a great heat conductor, helping to release heat faster and keep temperatures down. Many high-performance gaming laptops combine aluminum in the chassis for both aesthetic and useful reasons. The material provides a premium, sturdy build that also resists wear and tear, giving better long-term durability.

Pros:

- Excellent heat escape, keeping the laptop cooler.
- More durable and immune to wear and tear.
- Offers a premium look and feel, often with a sleek, modern design.

Cons:

- More expensive than plastic.

- Can be heavier, based on the thickness of the aluminum used.
- Can be more prone to dents and scratches than plastic.

For gamers who prioritize durability, cooling, and premium build quality, aluminum is generally the better pick. However, plastic builds can still be a viable option for gamers on a budget, given the cooling system and overall design are well-executed.

Battery Life: How to Balance Power with Portability

Battery life is another crucial consideration when choosing a gaming laptop. While gaming laptops are usually known for their high-power consumption, improvements in power management and battery technology have made it possible for gaming laptops to offer more reasonable battery life.

However, the powerful components that are essential for gaming—such as high-performance GPUs and CPUs—tend to drain battery life quickly, so it's important to strike the right balance between power and travel.

How Long Should Battery Life Last for a Gaming Laptop?

The battery life of a gaming laptop can vary significantly based on the specifications and power management features. Most gaming laptops are meant to last between 4 to 6 hours during light use, such as web browsing or watching videos. However, when gaming, battery life usually drops much faster.

1. Gaming Use: During gaming sessions, expect around 1.5 to 3 hours of battery life, based on the game's intensity and the laptop's battery capacity. More demanding games like Cyberpunk 2077 or Red Dead Redemption 2 will likely drain the battery faster than less graphically intensive titles.

2. *Non-Gaming Use:* For tasks like web browsing, word processing, and media consumption, a gaming laptop can last up to 5 to 8 hours, based on the configuration and how well power management is applied.

Battery life is one of the major trade-offs when choosing a gaming laptop, as the high-performance components take a lot of power. If you plan to game on the go or without access to a power outlet, it's important to consider a laptop with a larger battery or efficient power-saving features.

Tips for Maximizing Battery Performance

While gaming laptops are often power-hungry, there are several ways to improve battery life, even when you're gaming or using demanding applications:

1. *Adjust Power Settings:* Many gaming computers come with built-in power-saving modes. Adjusting your laptop's power settings can help conserve battery life when you're not gaming or performing demanding jobs. Lowering screen brightness and switching to power-saving mode can extend battery life during non-intensive tasks.

2. Close Background apps: Running multiple apps in the background while gaming can significantly impact battery performance. Close any unnecessary apps and processes to reduce power consumption and ensure the laptop focuses its energy on games.

3. Use Integrated Graphics: Some gaming laptops allow you to switch between the dedicated GPU (used for gaming) and integrated graphics (used for regular chores). Using integrated graphics for non-gaming activities can conserve battery life.

4. Disable Unnecessary Features: Disable power-hungry features such as RGB lights, Wi-Fi, Bluetooth, and high refresh rates when you're not gaming. These tools can drain battery life even when you're not actively using them.

5. Invest in a High-Capacity Power Bank: If you're planning to game while on the go, carrying a high-capacity portable power bank can help keep your gaming laptop charged during long trips or while flying. Ensure that the power bank has enough energy to power your laptop.

In conclusion, while gaming laptops usually don't excel in battery life compared to ultra books or lightweight laptops, there are ways to make the most out of your battery. A laptop with a bigger battery capacity, coupled with effective power management techniques, can provide a balance between performance and portability, making it more feasible to game on the go.

Chapter 3: Gaming Laptops for Every Budget

When looking for a gaming laptop, one of the first things to consider is your budget. Gaming laptops come in a wide range of prices, and it's important to know what to expect at different price points. Whether you're on a tight budget or looking for a premium machine, there's a game laptop that fits your needs. In this chapter, we'll break down the choices available for different budgets, starting with affordable models and moving into the mid-range.

Budget Gaming Laptops (Under $800)

For many gamers, finding a gaming laptop under $800 can be a challenge, especially if you want good performance and a smooth gaming experience. However, there are plenty of choices in this price range that can handle older titles or less graphically demanding games. While these laptops may not offer the same high-end speed as pricier models, they still provide solid gameplay for casual gamers or those on a tight budget.

What to Expect at This Price Range

At this price point, you won't get the high-end specifications found in more expensive models, but there are still some good options for budget-conscious gamers. Here's what you can expect from a game laptop under $800:

1. Graphics Card:

Most budget gaming laptops in this range will feature an entry-level or mid-range GPU, such as the NVIDIA GTX 1650 or the AMD Radeon RX 560X. While these GPUs can run many games at medium settings, you may have to lower the graphics settings or resolution to achieve smooth gameplay in more demanding titles.

2. Processor:

Budget game laptops are usually equipped with Intel Core i5 or AMD Ryzen 5 processors. While these CPUs are not as powerful as the higher-end i7/i9 or

Ryzen 7/9 chips, they can still handle casual gaming and everyday jobs with ease. Expect performance to be good for less resource-heavy games.

3. RAM:

8GB of RAM is usually the standard for budget gaming laptops, which is enough for most games and general multitasking. However, you might find some models with 4GB of RAM, which could be limiting for current games.

4. Storage:

In this price range, you'll often find laptops with traditional hard disk drives (HDDs) or hybrid drives, though some may come with solid-state drives (SSDs) for faster start times. You'll likely get around 256GB of SSD storage, which is fine for a few games, but may require additional storage solutions if you plan to store a large library of games.

5. Display:

Expect to find 15.6-inch Full HD screens with a 60Hz refresh rate. While this isn't the best display for fast-paced gaming, it's fine for more casual gaming sessions.

Top Budget Models and What They Offer

Here are some of the best budget gaming laptops under $800, each giving good performance for their price:

1. Acer Nitro 5

- CPU: Intel Core i5-10300H or AMD Ryzen 5 3550H
- GPU: NVIDIA GTX 1650
- RAM: 8GB
- Storage: 256GB SSD
- Display: 15.6-inch Full HD, 60Hz

Pros: Solid build quality, decent GPU for the price, good cooling system

Cons: Display refresh rate is smaller than higher-end models

2. Lenovo Legion 5

- CPU: AMD Ryzen 5 4600H
- GPU: NVIDIA GTX 1650 Ti
- RAM: 8GB
- Storage: 512GB SSD
- Display: 15.6-inch Full HD, 60Hz

Pros: Great value for speed, quiet cooling, durable build

Cons: Limited display frame rate

3. HP Pavilion Gaming Laptop

- CPU: Intel Core i5-9300H
- GPU: NVIDIA GTX 1650

- RAM: 8GB
- Storage: 512GB SSD
- Display: 15.6-inch Full HD, 60Hz

Pros: Budget-friendly with good gaming performance

Cons: Less expensive build quality, average display

While these cheap models can handle a wide range of games at medium settings, keep in mind that they won't run the latest AAA titles at ultra settings. These computers are ideal for casual gamers or those who don't mind lowering settings for smoother gameplay.

Mid-Range Gaming Laptops ($800 - $1500)

If you're looking for a gaming laptop that offers a better balance of performance and price, the $800 to $1500 range is where you'll find the sweet spot. Laptops in this price range offer more powerful

CPUs, better GPUs, and higher-quality displays, allowing you to play the latest AAA games at high settings without breaking the bank. They also tend to have better build quality and more premium functions compared to budget models.

Finding the Sweet Spot for Performance and Price

Gaming laptops in the $800 to $1500 range hit the ideal balance between performance and cost. Here's what you can usually expect from laptops in this price range:

1. Graphics Card:

Most mid-range laptops come with more powerful GPUs like the NVIDIA GTX 1660 Ti, RTX 2060, or the AMD Radeon RX 5600M. These GPUs can handle modern games at high settings and higher frame rates, making them great choices for gamers who want solid performance without spending over $1500.

2. Processor:

Mid-range game laptops are equipped with more powerful processors such as Intel Core i7 or AMD Ryzen 7 chips. These CPUs can handle difficult gaming and multitasking scenarios with ease, giving you better overall performance for both gaming and productivity tasks.

3. RAM:

At this price point, you'll usually find gaming laptops with 16GB of RAM, which is ideal for gaming, streaming, and multitasking. Having more RAM means that your laptop can handle more background processes without affecting gaming performance.

4. Storage:

Expect to see 512GB SSDs, or sometimes even 1TB SSDs in mid-range gaming computers. This allows for fast load times, quick system boot-ups, and sufficient room for several large games. Some models may even feature dual-storage options, with an SSD for the operating system and an HDD for extra game storage.

5. Display:

Mid-range gaming laptops generally feature Full HD (1920x1080) displays with higher refresh rates, usually around 120Hz or 144Hz, which is important for smoother, more responsive gameplay. Some models may even offer 4K displays, although this is usually reserved for the higher end of the price range.

6. Build Quality:

Laptops in this range tend to have sturdier, more premium builds, often using metal frames instead of plastic. The general aesthetic is often sleeker and more refined compared to budget models, with better cooling solutions and more comfortable keyboards for long game sessions.

Top Mid-Range Models and What They Offer

Here are a few of the best mid-range gaming laptops between $800 and $1500, each giving excellent performance for their price:

1. ASUS ROG Strix G15

- CPU: AMD Ryzen 7 5800H
- GPU: NVIDIA RTX 3060
- RAM: 16GB
- Storage: 512GB SSD
- Display: 15.6-inch Full HD, 144Hz

Pros: Excellent GPU speed, solid battery life, great for high settings

Cons: The fan noise can be a bit loud under load

2. MSI GF65 Thin

- CPU: Intel Core i7-10750H
- GPU: NVIDIA RTX 2060
- RAM: 16GB
- Storage: 512GB SSD

- Display: 15.6-inch Full HD, 144Hz

Pros: Good build quality, smooth 144Hz gameplay

Cons: Plastic build, could benefit from better battery life

3. Dell G5 15

- CPU: Intel Core i7-10750H
- GPU: NVIDIA GTX 1660 Ti
- RAM: 16GB
- Storage: 512GB SSD
- Display: 15.6-inch Full HD, 120Hz

Pros: Good value for speed, solid cooling system

Cons: Heavier than some competitors

These mid-range laptops offer an excellent balance of speed, features, and price. They're capable of running modern games at high settings, giving high frame rates and solid graphics performance, and are perfect for gamers who want a great experience without spending on top-tier, premium models.

Recommended Mid-Range Models ($800 - $1500)

Mid-range gaming laptops offer a great balance between price and ability. In this price range, you can find laptops that handle current AAA games at high settings, provide excellent build quality, and come with features that elevate the overall gaming experience. For gamers who want high-end performance without the premium price tag, mid-range laptops are the best choice.

Best Features You'll Get at This Price Point

Gaming laptops in the $800 to $1500 range come with major improvements over budget models. Here's what you can usually expect from a mid-range gaming laptop:

1. Graphics Card:

Mid-range laptops are equipped with more powerful GPUs such as the NVIDIA RTX 2060, 3060, or the AMD Radeon RX 6600M. These GPUs offer great performance in current games and can handle 1080p gaming at high or ultra settings. They also support ray tracing and other advanced graphical features, making them perfect for more demanding games.

2. Processor:

Expect to see Intel Core i7 or AMD Ryzen 7 processors in this price band. These CPUs provide the extra power needed to handle gaming, multitasking, and content production without bottlenecks. These processors are excellent for gaming and demanding applications, giving better performance over the i5 or Ryzen 5 options found in budget laptops.

3. RAM:

With 16GB of RAM, mid-range laptops allow you to run games and apps smoothly, even with multiple programs open at once. This is the ideal amount of memory for gaming and streaming, allowing you to switch between tasks without major performance drops.

4. Storage:

Mid-range gaming laptops typically feature fast 512GB or 1TB SSDs, providing adequate storage for large game libraries and reducing load times. SSDs are important for quick boot-up times and for reducing game load times, making a noticeable difference in overall performance.

5. Display:

In this price range, you'll often find Full HD (1920x1080) screens with high refresh rates (120Hz, 144Hz, or even 165Hz). These higher refresh rates are important for smooth and responsive gameplay, especially in fast-paced games like first-person shooters or racing games. Many mid-range gaming laptops also offer IPS screens for better color accuracy and wider viewing angles.

Top Recommended Mid-Range Models and What They Offer

Here are a few of the top mid-range gaming laptops that strike a great balance between speed and price:

1. ASUS ROG Strix G15

- CPU: AMD Ryzen 7 5800H
- GPU: NVIDIA GeForce RTX 3060
- RAM: 16GB
- Storage: 512GB SSD
- Display: 15.6-inch Full HD, 144Hz

Pros: Excellent build quality, powerful CPU and GPU mix, solid cooling system

Cons: Can get a bit loud under heavy load

2. MSI GF65 Thin

- CPU: Intel Core i7-10750H
- GPU: NVIDIA GeForce RTX 2060
- RAM: 16GB
- Storage: 512GB SSD
- Display: 15.6-inch Full HD, 144Hz

Pros: Great value for speed, sleek and portable design, solid build quality

Cons: Average battery life, limited port choices

3. Dell G5 15

- CPU: Intel Core i7-10750H
- GPU: NVIDIA GeForce GTX 1660 Ti
- RAM: 16GB
- Storage: 512GB SSD
- Display: 15.6-inch Full HD, 120Hz

Pros: Good build quality, great cooling system, comfortable keyboard

Cons: Slightly heavy, can be loud under load

These mid-range laptops provide an excellent balance of power, portability, and affordability, making them great for gamers who want good performance without overspending on top-tier models.

High-End Gaming Laptops ($1500 and Above)

For gamers who want the absolute best performance and features, high-end gaming laptops are the go-to pick. These laptops are packed with top-of-the-line components and offer cutting-edge technology to ensure the best possible game and multitasking experience. Whether you're playing the latest AAA games, experiencing virtual reality, or making content, high-end gaming laptops are built to handle it all.

Best Features You'll Get at This Price Point

High-end gaming laptops provide unmatched performance and visual quality, making them ideal for those who expect the best. Here's what you can expect:

1. Graphics Card:

At this price range, you'll get top-tier GPUs like the NVIDIA GeForce RTX 3070, 3080, or the latest 4090, or AMD Radeon RX 6800M. These GPUs allow you to run current games at ultra settings with high frame rates, even in 4K. They also support real-time ray tracing for ultra-realistic lighting, reflections, and shadows, taking your game experience to the next level.

2. Processor:

High-end game laptops are equipped with the most powerful CPUs, including Intel Core i9 or AMD Ryzen 9 processors. These computers can handle the most demanding games, multitasking, content creation, and even VR, ensuring smooth performance no matter what you're doing.

3. RAM:

Expect 16GB to 32GB of RAM, offering ample memory for gaming, multitasking, video editing, and running resource-heavy applications. This amount of RAM ensures you can run modern games at high settings while streaming, editing videos, or using other apps simultaneously without any slowdowns.

4. Storage:

High-end laptops come with large SSDs (1TB or more), giving plenty of room for your game library and fast load times. Some models may even feature dual storage solutions, combining a fast SSD for system and game storage with a larger HDD for extra file storage.

5. Display:

In the high-end section, you'll often find 4K displays or Full HD displays with refresh rates of 240Hz or even 360Hz. These displays ensure smooth and responsive gameplay, with vivid colors and ultra-clear graphics. Some high-end laptops feature OLED or mini-LED displays for better color accuracy and contrast.

6. Build Quality and Cooling:

Premium game laptops often feature metal chassis made from materials like aluminum or magnesium alloy. These materials are more sturdy, heat-resistant, and give the laptop a premium feel. High-end models also feature advanced cooling systems, such as vapor chambers, liquid cooling, or multiple fans, to keep your laptop cool during intense game sessions.

Premium Models That Offer Cutting-Edge Performance

For those ready to invest in the highest quality, these premium models provide the cutting-edge performance and features that make them stand out from the competition:

1. Razer Blade 15 Advanced

- CPU: Intel Core i9-11900H
- GPU: NVIDIA GeForce RTX 3080
- RAM: 32GB
- Storage: 1TB SSD
- Display: 15.6-inch 4K OLED, 60Hz

Pros: Ultra-slim design, top-tier GPU and CPU mix, stunning 4K OLED display

Cons: Expensive, shorter battery life due to powerful components

2. Alienware X17

- CPU: Intel Core i9-11980HK
- GPU: NVIDIA GeForce RTX 3080
- RAM: 32GB
- Storage: 1TB SSD
- Display: 17.3-inch Full HD, 360Hz

Pros: Excellent cooling, powerful GPU, and high refresh rate for competitive games

Cons: Heavy and big, high price

3. Asus ROG Zephyrus G15

- CPU: AMD Ryzen 9 5900HS
- GPU: NVIDIA GeForce RTX 3080
- RAM: 32GB
- Storage: 1TB SSD
- Display: 15.6-inch QHD, 165Hz

Pros: Lightweight, powerful, exceptional battery life for game laptops

Cons: No webcam, limited upgrade choices

These high-end models are made to provide maximum gaming performance, ultra-fast frame rates, beautiful displays, and seamless multitasking. They're great for serious gamers, content creators, and anyone who demands the best performance and quality from their laptop.

In summary, gaming computers come in all shapes, sizes, and price points. Whether you're on a tight budget or looking for the most powerful machine on the market, there's a game laptop that fits your needs. By considering your budget, performance standards, and desired features, you can find a gaming laptop that offers the best value and meets your gaming needs.

Chapter 4: Choosing a Gaming Laptop Based on Your Gaming Style

Choosing the right gaming laptop isn't just about specifications—it's also about understanding your gaming style and needs. Different types of gamers have different goals, and what works for a casual gamer might not work for a competitive player or a content creator. In this chapter, we'll break down the best gaming laptops based on three popular gaming styles: casual gaming, competitive gaming (esports), and content creation/streaming. Each part will help guide you in selecting the ideal laptop for your gaming preferences.

Casual Gamers: Finding a Laptop for Casual Gaming and Entertainment

Casual gamers are those who enjoy playing games for fun, without the need for ultra-high performance. They may not require top-tier hardware or the highest frame rates, but they still want a laptop that offers a smooth and enjoyable gaming experience. Casual gaming includes titles like Fortnite, Minecraft, League of Legends, and other games that are not as demanding on gear compared to AAA titles.

What You Need for Games Like Fortnite, Minecraft, and League of Legends

For casual gaming, you don't need a laptop with bleeding-edge components, but you do need a system that can handle everyday games with ease. Here's what you should value when shopping for a gaming laptop for casual games:

1. Graphics Card:

For casual gaming, a mid-range or entry-level GPU like the NVIDIA GTX 1650 or GTX 1660 Ti, or an AMD Radeon RX 5600M, is more than suitable. These GPUs can run popular social games like Minecraft, Fortnite, and League of Legends at 1080p with smooth frame rates. More graphically demanding games might require changes to settings, but these GPUs can easily handle titles with moderate graphical needs.

2. Processor:

A quad-core or hexa-core processor, such as an Intel Core i5 or AMD Ryzen 5, will provide plenty of power for casual gameplay. These CPUs are great for running lighter games without experiencing any bottlenecks. You can also multitask with ease— whether it's browsing the web, watching movies, or chatting on Discord while gaming.

3. RAM:

8GB of RAM is usually enough for casual gaming. It will allow you to run the game you want while having other applications open in the background, such as web browsers, streaming services, or music players. If you plan to use the laptop for other multitasking needs like video editing or having multiple apps going, consider opting for 16GB of RAM.

4. Storage:

For casual gaming, a 256GB or 512GB SSD is best. The SSD will reduce load times greatly, offering faster boot-ups and game loading. You might not need the largest storage choice, as casual games like Minecraft or League of Legends don't require vast amounts of space, but having enough room for a few games and media files is key. For budget options, hybrid storage setups (SSD + HDD) are popular and can help maximize storage without sacrificing speed.

5. Display:

A 15.6-inch Full HD display (1920x1080) with a 60Hz refresh rate is more than enough for casual games. The focus here is not on ultra-high refresh rates or 4K resolution, but rather a solid, clear display that offers vibrant colors for a fun gaming experience. An IPS display will give you better color accuracy and wider viewing angles, which is great for games that feature vibrant visuals.

6. Battery Life:

Casual gamers are more likely to play while plugged in, but longer battery life is still a consideration for those who game on the go. Laptops with around 5-8 hours of battery life will provide enough time for gaming during short sessions or while moving. Recommended Laptops for Casual Gamers

1. Acer Nitro 5

- CPU: Intel Core i5-9300H
- GPU: NVIDIA GTX 1650
- RAM: 8GB
- Storage: 512GB SSD
- Display: 15.6-inch Full HD, 60Hz

Pros: Affordable, decent gaming performance for casual games, good cooling

Cons: Basic device, bulky design

2. Lenovo Legion 5

- CPU: AMD Ryzen 5 4600H
- GPU: NVIDIA GTX 1650 Ti
- RAM: 8GB
- Storage: 512GB SSD

- Display: 15.6-inch Full HD, 60Hz

Pros: Great performance for its price, great build quality

Cons: A bit heavy for a 15.6-inch laptop

3. HP Pavilion Gaming Laptop

- CPU: Intel Core i5-9300H
- GPU: NVIDIA GTX 1650
- RAM: 8GB
- Storage: 512GB SSD
- Display: 15.6-inch Full HD, 60Hz

Pros: Decent graphics speed, budget-friendly

Cons: Average power life, lower-end display

These laptops are affordable and great for casual gamers who play moderately demanding games or enjoy lighter titles like Fortnite or Minecraft.

Competitive/Esports Gamers: Laptops for High-Speed, Professional Gaming

Competitive gamers or esports players need a gaming laptop that can offer high speeds, ultra-smooth graphics, and precise controls. Laptops in this category need to be able to handle fast-paced games like Counter-Strike: Global Offensive, Apex Legends, Valorant, or Call of Duty: Warzone with ease, giving a competitive edge.

The Need for Speed: High Refresh Rates and Low Latency

When it comes to competitive gaming, speed and precision are important. To get the best out of high-speed games, you'll need the following features:

1. High Refresh Rates:

A high refresh rate monitor (120Hz, 144Hz, or 240Hz) is important for esports players. These displays provide smoother gameplay and allow you to see more frames per second, which is important for fast-paced games. High refresh rates reduce motion blur and improve accuracy, giving you a competitive edge in games that demand quick reflexes, such as first-person shooters and multiplayer online battle arenas (MOBAs).

2. Low Latency:

In competitive games, input lag can mean the difference between winning and losing. Low latency guarantees that your commands are registered instantly. High-end gaming laptops built for esports typically come with response times of 1-3 milliseconds, ensuring there's no delay between your inputs and what happens on-screen.

3. High-Performance CPU and GPU:

For esports, a laptop with at least an Intel Core i7 or AMD Ryzen 7 processor is needed to keep up with fast-paced gameplay. The GPU should be an NVIDIA GeForce RTX 3060, 3070, or 3080, or an AMD

Radeon RX 6700M or 6800M, to handle high settings and fast frame rates while reducing input lag to a minimum.

Recommended Esports Laptops

1. Alienware m15 R4

- CPU: Intel Core i7-10870H
- GPU: NVIDIA GeForce RTX 3070
- RAM: 16GB
- Storage: 512GB SSD
- Display: 15.6-inch Full HD, 144Hz

Pros: Excellent GPU, fast update rate, high-quality build

Cons: Expensive, heavy

2. ASUS ROG Strix G15

- CPU: AMD Ryzen 7 5800H
- GPU: NVIDIA GeForce RTX 3060

- RAM: 16GB
- Storage: 512GB SSD
- Display: 15.6-inch Full HD, 144Hz

Pros: Great performance for games, sleek design, high refresh rate

Cons: Battery life could be better

3. MSI GL65 Leopard

- CPU: Intel Core i7-10750H
- GPU: NVIDIA GeForce RTX 2060
- RAM: 16GB
- Storage: 512GB SSD
- Display: 15.6-inch Full HD, 144Hz

Pros: Affordable for the efficiency, good cooling
Cons: Display could be better in terms of color clarity

These laptops provide high refresh rates, fast processors, and powerful GPUs—perfect for competitive gamers who need to perform at their best in esports contests or online games.

Content Creators and Streamers: Gaming Laptops for Multi-Tasking and Streaming

For content creators and streamers, a gaming laptop needs to do more than just run games—it needs to handle multi-tasking, video editing, and live streaming while keeping smooth performance. Whether you're streaming your gameplay on platforms like Twitch or YouTube, or making video content, having the right equipment is key to delivering quality streams and videos.

Key Features for Streamers and Content Creators

1. Powerful CPU and GPU:

Content creation needs powerful components to handle demanding tasks like video rendering, live streaming, and gaming. A laptop with an Intel Core i7 or i9, or an AMD Ryzen 7/9 processor, paired with an NVIDIA GeForce RTX 3060/3070 or AMD Radeon RX 6700M, will allow you to handle multiple tasks without any hiccups.

2. RAM:

For seamless multitasking, 16GB or 32GB of RAM is best. Streamers often run multiple apps simultaneously, such as OBS for streaming, Discord for voice chat, and video editing software. More RAM guarantees smooth performance even while running resource-heavy programs.

3. Storage:

For content creators, having plenty of fast storage is important. A 512GB or 1TB SSD is suggested for storing your games, media files, and editing software. A larger SSD allows for faster load times and provides enough room for large video files and high-resolution assets.

4. Display:

A high-quality display is important for content creation and streaming. Look for a 15.6-inch or 17.3-inch monitor with a high refresh rate (120Hz or 144Hz) and good color accuracy (IPS or OLED). A 4K display is even better for detailed video editing and correct color work.

Recommended Laptops for Streamers and Content Creators

1. Razer Blade 15 Advanced

- CPU: Intel Core i9-11900H
- GPU: NVIDIA GeForce RTX 3080
- RAM: 32GB
- Storage: 1TB SSD
- Display: 15.6-inch 4K OLED, 60Hz

Pros: Premium design, stunning display, top-tier GPU and CPU for both games and content creation

Cons: Expensive, shorter battery life

2. Asus ROG Zephyrus G14

- CPU: AMD Ryzen 9 5900HS
- GPU: NVIDIA GeForce RTX 3060
- RAM: 16GB
- Storage: 1TB SSD
- Display: 14-inch QHD, 120Hz

Pros: Lightweight, great performance, excellent for games and streaming

Cons: Smaller screen for content creation, no webcam

3. MSI Creator 15

- CPU: Intel Core i7-10870H
- GPU: NVIDIA GeForce RTX 3070
- RAM: 16GB
- Storage: 512GB SSD

- Display: 15.6-inch 4K, 60Hz

Pros: Excellent for content creation, powerful speed, high-resolution display

Cons: Heavier, more expensive than other game laptops

These laptops offer the power and features needed for streamers and content makers to game, edit, and stream seamlessly. Whether you're making videos, streaming live, or editing high-definition content, these machines provide everything you need for high-quality production.

Balancing Gaming with Video Editing and Streaming Needs

For many gamers, the line between gaming and content making is blurred. Whether you're streaming your gameplay, creating video guides, or editing highlights, having a gaming laptop that can handle both gaming and content creation is important. The best laptops for this dual-purpose use not only provide excellent gaming performance but also offer the power and efficiency needed for video editing, live streaming, and other creative chores.

Features to Look for in a Laptop for Content Creation

1. Powerful Processor (CPU)

Video editing and streaming require a robust CPU to process and render large video files fast. Look for computers with at least an Intel Core i7 or AMD Ryzen 7 processor. For heavy-duty tasks, Intel Core i9 or AMD Ryzen 9 CPUs offer even more power, allowing smoother performance during multitasking, video editing, and live streaming.

2. High-Performance Graphics Card (GPU)

While the GPU is crucial for games, it's equally important for video editing and streaming. The NVIDIA GeForce RTX series or AMD Radeon RX series are optimal picks for content creators. These GPUs not only enhance game visuals but also accelerate rendering tasks in video editing software like Adobe Premiere Pro or DaVinci Resolve. For 3D rendering and other graphics-heavy tasks, a high-end GPU is essential.

3. Sufficient RAM

A content maker needs ample RAM for multitasking—streaming, editing, and gaming simultaneously. 16GB of RAM is the bare minimum, but 32GB of RAM is ideal if you're handling bigger video files or working with more demanding editing software. More RAM allows for smoother multitasking, with less lag when switching between apps.

4. Fast Storage (SSD)

For video makers and streamers, fast storage is a must. 512GB to 1TB SSDs offer the speed needed to store big video files and load programs quickly. SSDs are much faster than standard HDDs and allow for smoother video editing workflows, reduced render times, and quicker game load times. If you plan on storing a lot of raw footage or games, consider models that feature dual storage—an SSD for the operating system and important files, and an HDD for larger files and media.

5. High-Quality Display

When editing videos or live streaming, color accuracy and screen clarity are important. Look for laptops with IPS screens for better color reproduction and wider viewing angles. A laptop with a 4K display is even better for accurate color grading and detailed editing. Additionally, if you plan to stream or record content, having a display with a high refresh rate (120Hz or 144Hz) is helpful for a smoother experience when gaming or editing.

6. Long Battery Life

While gaming laptops tend to have lower battery life due to their high-performance components, content makers who also game on the go should look for laptops with better battery management. Ideally, 5 to 8 hours of battery life should serve for light editing or streaming sessions, though heavy video editing or gaming will still drain the battery faster.

Recommended Laptops for Content Creation and Streaming

1. Razer Blade 15 Advanced

- CPU: Intel Core i9-11900H
- GPU: NVIDIA GeForce RTX 3080
- RAM: 32GB
- Storage: 1TB SSD
- Display: 15.6-inch 4K OLED, 60Hz

Pros: Outstanding build quality, excellent display for video editing, top-tier GPU and CPU for games and content creation

Cons: High price, shorter battery life under heavy load

2. Asus ROG Zephyrus G14

- CPU: AMD Ryzen 9 5900HS
- GPU: NVIDIA GeForce RTX 3060
- RAM: 16GB
- Storage: 1TB SSD
- Display: 14-inch QHD, 120Hz

Pros: Lightweight, powerful for both games and content creation, solid battery life

Cons: Smaller screen, no webcam

3. MSI Creator 15

- CPU: Intel Core i7-10870H
- GPU: NVIDIA GeForce RTX 3070
- RAM: 16GB
- Storage: 512GB SSD
- Display: 15.6-inch 4K, 60Hz

Pros: Designed for content creators, great display for video editing, strong GPU

Cons: Heavier, more expensive than gaming computers with similar specs

These laptops are excellent choices for gamers who also want to make content. They provide the speed, display quality, and multitasking capability needed for video editing, streaming, and gaming, making them perfect for those balancing both gaming and creative work.

VR Gamers: Laptops for Virtual Reality Gaming

Virtual reality (VR) gaming has grown greatly in popularity, giving gamers an unparalleled level of immersion. However, VR gaming puts a high demand on system resources. The best VR game computers need to support high frame rates, low latency, and powerful graphical rendering to ensure a smooth, immersive experience. To run VR titles like Half-Life: Alyx or Beat Saber, a laptop must be VR-ready, meaning it meets the specific standards needed to run VR headsets like the Oculus Rift, HTC Vive, or Valve Index.

What Makes a Laptop VR-Ready?

1. High-Performance GPU

A VR-ready laptop must be equipped with a strong GPU, such as the NVIDIA RTX 3060 or higher, or AMD Radeon RX 6700M or higher. These GPUs ensure that VR games are rendered at a high frame rate (at least 90Hz) for a smooth experience. A powerful GPU also supports the rendering of high-quality visuals needed for VR, without causing lag or stuttering, which can lead to nausea or discomfort.

2. Fast Processor (CPU)

A fast CPU is essential for VR gaming, as it handles the complex computations needed by VR environments. Look for computers with at least an Intel Core i7 or AMD Ryzen 7 processor. VR experiences are highly demanding, and having a multi-core processor ensures smooth performance during gameplay and lowers the chances of frame drops.

3. Sufficient RAM

VR gaming needs a significant amount of memory to keep the experience fluid. 16GB of RAM is the minimum, though 32GB is suggested for an optimal experience. More RAM allows for seamless multitasking while running VR apps, games, and background tasks.

4. Low Latency and High Refresh Rates

For VR gaming, low latency is important. Latency refers to the delay between your actions and what you see on the screen, and high latency can cause dizziness or motion sickness in VR. Ensure the laptop has a high refresh rate (at least 90Hz or higher) to meet the VR headset's requirements. VR headsets demand a consistent frame rate to avoid lag and keep immersion.

5. HDMI/DisplayPort Connectivity

VR headsets require a physical connection to the laptop, usually via HDMI or DisplayPort. Many VR-ready laptops include dedicated ports for these connections, ensuring that you can connect your VR headset without any problems. Additionally, some models come with USB 3.0 or USB-C ports for extra VR accessories, such as sensors or external cameras.

Best Laptops for Oculus, HTC Vive, and More

Here are some of the best laptops for VR gaming, capable of handling demanding VR experiences and having excellent performance across the board:

1. Alienware m15 R4

- **CPU:** Intel Core i7-10870H

- **GPU:** NVIDIA GeForce RTX 3070
- RAM: 16GB
- Storage: 512GB SSD
- Display: 15.6-inch Full HD, 144Hz

Pros: Excellent for VR gaming, smooth speed with high-end GPU, good cooling system

Cons: Expensive, heavy for a 15.6-inch laptop

2. Asus ROG Strix G15

- CPU: AMD Ryzen 7 5800H
- GPU: NVIDIA GeForce RTX 3060
- RAM: 16GB
- Storage: 512GB SSD
- Display: 15.6-inch Full HD, 144Hz

Pros: Good value for VR games, sleek design, fast refresh rate

Cons: No webcam, might struggle with ultra-high levels for VR games

3. MSI GE76 Raider

- CPU: Intel Core i9-11980HK
- GPU: NVIDIA GeForce RTX 3080
- RAM: 32GB
- Storage: 1TB SSD
- Display: 17.3-inch 4K, 120Hz

Pros: Incredible VR performance, big display for immersive VR experiences, powerful GPU

Cons: Heavy and big, short battery life

These laptops are specifically built to meet the demands of VR gaming, giving a smooth, immersive experience with high-quality visuals, low latency, and powerful performance. Whether you're using the Oculus Rift, HTC Vive, or any other VR headset, these models will ensure your VR game experience is as seamless as possible.

By understanding the specific features that matter most to each type of gamer—casual, competitive, content creator, or VR enthusiast—you can make an informed choice that fits your needs and ensures you get the best possible gaming experience.

Chapter 5: How to Compare Gaming Laptops

When you're looking to buy a gaming laptop, it's important to understand how to compare different models to ensure you get the best performance for your budget. Performance can be affected by various things, including the CPU, GPU, RAM, storage, and cooling system. In this chapter, we'll dive into how to measure gaming laptops, how to read and compare benchmarks, and what real-world performance looks like for gaming laptops.

Benchmarking Performance: Understanding Game Benchmarks and Reviews

One of the most effective ways to assess gaming laptops is by using benchmarks. Benchmarks are speed tests that measure a laptop's ability to run certain tasks, like gaming. These tests are performed using specific games or software, and the results help to determine how well a laptop handles demanding applications.

How to Read Benchmark Results

When you look at gaming laptop benchmarks, the results usually come in the form of frame rates, also referred to as frames per second (FPS), as well as other key performance measures such as:

1. Frames Per Second (FPS):

FPS is one of the most important measures for gamers. It refers to the number of frames a laptop can render in one second. The higher the FPS, the smoother the game experience. For example:

- 30 FPS is the bare minimum for playing most games.
- 60 FPS is considered ideal for a smooth and enjoyable game experience.
- 120 FPS or higher is ideal for fast-paced games, especially in esports where every frame counts.

A higher FPS suggests better performance, but it's important to note that FPS can vary based on the settings (such as low, medium, or high graphics) and the resolution of the game.

2. Resolution:

When comparing benchmarks, it's important to pay attention to the resolution at which the test was run. Many benchmarks are run at 1080p (Full HD), but some may be tried at 1440p (QHD) or 4K. Higher resolutions take more processing power and can cause FPS to drop compared to testing at 1080p.

3. Graphics Settings:

Laptops may be tried at different graphics settings, such as low, medium, or ultra. If you want to know how a laptop works with the highest settings, look for benchmarks done at ultra settings. However, for smooth gaming, many players opt for medium or high settings, which provide a good mix between performance and visual fidelity.

4. Temperature and Throttling:

Benchmarking also measures how well a laptop handles heat. As powerful components like CPUs and GPUs are used during gaming, they create heat. The temperature is an important metric because if a laptop's cooling system isn't effective, it may experience thermal throttling—where the processor slows down to avoid overheating, negatively affecting performance.

Comparing Different Laptops for the Same Game

When comparing gaming laptops for the same game, ensure that the tests were performed under similar conditions, including resolution, graphics settings, and the game's version. Here's how to do it:

1. Check the FPS at Specific Resolutions:

Always compare benchmarks at the same resolution (e.g., 1080p or 1440p) because different resolutions will affect speed. A laptop that works well at 1080p might struggle at 1440p or 4K.

2. Look at the Settings:

Ensure that the graphics options in the benchmark tests are the same. For instance, if you're comparing laptops using Shadow of the Tomb Raider, ensure that both laptops are tried at Ultra or High settings.

3. Consider the GPU:

The GPU is a big factor in gaming performance. For example, an NVIDIA RTX 3060 will perform better than a GTX 1650 in most current games. So, compare laptops with similar GPUs to get a true comparison of performance.

4. Use Multiple Game Benchmarks:

Don't just rely on one game for comparison. Some laptops may succeed at certain games while underperforming in others. Look for laptops that work consistently well across a variety of popular titles like Cyberpunk 2077, Red Dead Redemption 2, Fortnite, and Apex Legends.

5. Real-World vs Synthetic Benchmarks:

Synthetic benchmarks (like 3DMark and Cinebench) test a laptop's performance by running a number of standardized tasks that don't exactly replicate real-world gaming scenarios. Real-world benchmarks, on the other hand, are based on real gameplay. While fake benchmarks can show raw power, real-world benchmarks give you a better idea of how the laptop will perform in the games you play.

Real-World Performance: What to Expect When Gaming

While benchmarks provide important data, nothing beats real-world performance. The speed you experience when gaming will rely on various factors, such as game optimization, cooling, and how well the laptop handles multitasking during gaming.

Here's what to expect when gaming on a gaming laptop, based on different price ranges:

Budget Gaming Laptops (Under $800)

Laptops in this price range will allow you to play older or less demanding games at 1080p with medium settings. Games like Fortnite, Minecraft, and League of Legends will run smoothly at 60 FPS on medium settings. However, you may have to lower the resolution or graphics settings for more demanding AAA games like Cyberpunk 2077 or Red Dead Redemption 2.

You might expect 30-60 FPS on high settings for older games and 20-40 FPS for newer, more graphically intensive games at lower settings.

Mid-Range Gaming Laptops ($800 - $1500)

In the mid-range, gaming laptops are capable of running most current titles at high settings at 1080p, with frame rates around 60-100 FPS. Laptops with GPUs like the NVIDIA RTX 3060 or RTX 3070 will perform well in both AAA games and competitive titles like Valorant, Call of Duty: Warzone, and Apex Legends.

For esports games, you can expect 144Hz or higher refresh rates, which is great for competitive gaming. For AAA games, expect 50-70 FPS on ultra settings at 1080p, and 40-50 FPS at 1440p.

High-End Gaming Laptops ($1500 and Above)

High-end gaming laptops come with the best graphics cards, processors, and displays, allowing you to enjoy games at 4K, high refresh rates, and ultra settings. With an RTX 3080 or RTX 4090, you can expect 100+ FPS on ultra settings in most current AAA games, such as Cyberpunk 2077 or Red Dead Redemption 2. VR gaming also works excellently on these systems, delivering smooth, immersive experiences without lag or stuttering. These laptops are also capable of maintaining high frame rates in 4K resolution, though performance will vary based on the game and settings.

Key Takeaways:

1. FPS Expectations: Expect 60 FPS or higher on middle settings for budget laptops, 100 FPS or higher for mid-range laptops, and 120 FPS+ for high-end models.

2. Resolution and Settings: 1080p is the sweet spot for budget and mid-range models, while high-end versions handle 1440p and 4K well.

3. Game Performance: Competitive games like CS:GO or Valorant benefit most from high refresh rates (144Hz+), while AAA titles require a balance of high FPS and visual fidelity.

In summary, knowing gaming laptop performance involves looking at both benchmark results and real-world gaming scenarios. By analyzing FPS, resolution, graphics settings, and real-world performance, you can find the right laptop that fits your gaming needs. Keep in mind that high-end laptops offer the best performance but come at a premium price, while mid-range and cheap laptops can still provide a great gaming experience at more affordable prices.

Frame Rate vs. Graphics Settings

When choosing a gaming laptop, understanding the relationship between frame rate and graphics settings is important. Both elements greatly influence your gaming experience, but they often require a balance to achieve optimal performance.

Frame Rate (FPS) refers to how many frames your laptop can produce per second. A faster frame rate results in smoother, more responsive gameplay, especially in fast-paced games where every second counts. However, getting a high frame rate requires a strong Graphics Processing Unit (GPU) that can handle demanding graphical loads.

Graphics Settings, on the other hand, decide the visual quality of your game. Settings like texture quality, shadow quality, anti-aliasing, and draw distance all impact how the game looks, but they can also affect speed. Higher graphics settings look more realistic but require more GPU power, which can result in lower frame rates.

When gaming, frame rate and graphics settings go hand in hand: you need enough graphical power to achieve smooth frame rates while still having visually appealing graphics.

For example, 60 FPS at medium settings is great for many gamers, but 30 FPS with ultra settings might not provide the same experience in terms of responsiveness, especially for competitive gaming.

1. Frame Rate vs. Graphics Quality in Gaming:

a). 60 FPS vs. Ultra Settings: Achieving 60 FPS with high settings is the goal for most gamers. This gives you smooth gameplay without losing too much visual fidelity. Laptops in the mid-range to high-end price points can handle this mix with ease for most games.

b). Frame Rate Dips and Graphics Settings:
In demanding games, if your frame rate goes below 30 FPS, it can result in choppy gameplay and lag. To keep smoother gameplay, you can lower graphics settings, which can increase FPS without sacrificing overall performance. Lowering shadows, texture quality, or anti-aliasing can greatly improve FPS.

2. *Optimizing Frame Rate for Competitive Gaming:*

For competitive gamers, smooth frame rates are important. In games like Fortnite or Apex Legends, 144Hz or 240Hz refresh rates are chosen because they ensure fast reactions and smooth motion. In these cases, lowering graphics settings to achieve higher frame rates is often necessary to keep a competitive advantage.

A 144Hz display on a laptop with an RTX 3060 can offer outstanding performance at high settings while keeping FPS above 100 for an ultra-smooth experience.

The Role of Optimizations in Popular Games Many modern games are highly optimized to run easily on a variety of systems, including gaming laptops. Developers use specific optimizations to make sure games work well on a wide range of hardware configurations.

These improvements may include dynamic resolution scaling, adaptive graphics settings, and frame rate caps.

1. *Dynamic Resolution Scaling:*

Some games use dynamic resolution scaling to change the resolution of the game in real-time based on performance. For example, in places with high graphical intensity, the resolution might drop slightly to keep a consistent frame rate, but when the scene becomes less demanding, the resolution will scale back up. This helps to balance speed with visual quality.

2. *Adaptive Graphics Settings:*

Many games allow you to change settings like shadows, texture quality, and post-processing effects based on the GPU's performance. This means that even if you have a less powerful GPU, you can still play the game easily by turning down certain graphics settings. Some games also have built-in presets like Low, Medium, and High settings, which change all graphical parameters automatically to fit your laptop's capabilities.

3. *Frame Rate Caps:*

Frame rate caps are often used in competitive games to prevent excessive power usage and to ensure stable performance. For example, games like CS:GO and League of Legends often cap frame rates at 120 FPS or 144 FPS to keep a stable, consistent gaming experience without overloading the system. This can also be useful if you want to save power or reduce heat generation during long gaming sessions. Optimized Games vs. Unoptimized Games:

Games like Fortnite, Apex Legends, and Valorant are highly optimized for gaming laptops and can run on a range of hardware configurations. You'll usually see stable frame rates even on lower-end models, thanks to optimizations.

On the other hand, some AAA games like Cyberpunk 2077 or Red Dead Redemption 2 are less optimized and demand higher-end hardware to achieve smooth gameplay, especially at ultra settings. If your laptop is struggling with these games, lowering graphics settings or allowing game-specific optimizations can help.

Long-Term Considerations: Will Your Laptop Last for Future Games?

When buying a gaming laptop, it's important to consider how future-proof your purchase is. The gaming industry is evolving quickly, with new games wanting increasingly powerful hardware. While you may be able to play today's games on your laptop with ease, you need to think about whether it will handle next-generation titles with the same level of speed. Here's how you can make sure your laptop stays capable in the years to come.

How to Future-Proof Your Purchase

1. Opt for a Powerful GPU:

The GPU is the heart of a gaming laptop, and it has the most significant effect on gaming performance. While mid-range GPUs like the RTX 3060 or RTX 3070 are excellent choices for current-generation games, if you want to future-proof your system, consider investing in an RTX 3080 or RTX 4090 (if within your budget). These GPUs are more likely to handle future games with demanding graphics, allowing you to enjoy high frame rates and ultra settings for years to come.

2. *Prioritize CPU Power:*

While the GPU is the most important factor for gaming, the CPU also plays a critical part, especially in CPU-intensive games. Intel Core i7 or AMD Ryzen 7 processors will handle today's games with ease, but for long-term performance, Intel Core i9 or AMD Ryzen 9 processors will provide the space for future titles. These CPUs offer more cores and threads, which are important for current and upcoming game engines that require more processing power.

3. *Increase RAM:*

For future-proofing, 16GB of RAM is a good baseline for gaming laptops, but 32GB will give you more room for multitasking and running more resource-intensive apps in parallel. As games become more complicated and require larger assets, more RAM ensures you won't run into performance bottlenecks.

4. *Solid Storage Options:*

Gaming laptops with 1TB SSDs are ideal for storing big games and ensuring quick load times. SSDs also help with multitasking, which is important for future-proofing when you're running multiple apps (e.g., streaming software, Discord, or video editing software). Dual storage options (SSD + HDD) are also great, as they provide both speed and ample storage room.

5. *High Refresh Rate Displays:*

While a 60Hz refresh rate may work for most gaming laptops, a 120Hz or 144Hz refresh rate will give you a better experience in high-speed games. If you want to enjoy the best visuals for competitive gaming, try 240Hz or 360Hz displays. These higher refresh rates are more future-proof, especially as games become more responsive and creators optimize games for higher frame rates.

6. Ensure Good Cooling and Battery Life:

More challenging games mean more heat. Choosing a laptop with a good cooling system will avoid thermal throttling and ensure consistent performance. Additionally, longer battery life is a good idea if you plan to game on the go or use your laptop for content creation.

What to Avoid:

Avoid buying the cheapest models with entry-level components if you're hoping to game at ultra settings in the future. Investing in a high-end GPU and powerful CPU today will save you from having to upgrade too soon.

- Not considering future software demands: As game development improves, future games may require more than what a laptop with older CPUs and GPUs can handle. It's best to plan ahead for future software needs.

Key Takeaways for Future-Proofing:

- Opt for high-end components like RTX 3080 or RTX 4090 for GPUs, Intel Core i9 or AMD Ryzen 9 processors, and 32GB of RAM for life.
- Choose 1TB SSD storage and favor high refresh rate displays for immersive gaming experiences.
- A solid cooling system and extended battery life will keep your laptop working well for longer.

By understanding how to compare gaming laptops based on benchmarks, real-world performance, and future gaming demands, you can make an informed decision when purchasing a laptop that will provide top-tier gaming experiences today and stay capable for years to come.

Chapter 6: Additional Features and Considerations

When it comes to choosing the perfect gaming laptop, performance is just one part of the decision-making process. To ensure you get the most out of your laptop, there are additional features and considerations you need to take in, such as port selection and cooling solutions. These factors play a crucial role in enhancing your gaming experience and ensuring the longevity of your laptop. In this chapter, we'll explore the importance of port selection and cooling solutions, two often-overlooked yet essential factors in choosing a game laptop.

Port Selection: Ensuring Your Laptop Has All the Right Ports

When you buy a gaming laptop, you don't just need it to run your games—you also need it to connect smoothly with other devices like monitors, external hard drives, gaming peripherals, and other accessories. Port selection is a key factor in ensuring your laptop meets all your needs, both for gaming and for everyday use.

USB-C, HDMI, Thunderbolt, and Other Essential Ports

1. USB-C:

USB-C has become the standard for high-speed data transfer and charging, and most modern gaming computers are equipped with at least one USB-C port. These ports offer fast data transfer speeds and can handle USB 3.1 or USB 3.2 for quick file transfers, external storage connections, and more.

USB-C ports are also capable of power delivery, meaning you can use them to charge your laptop (in addition to the normal charging port), which is especially useful when traveling or when you need to power your laptop from an external power bank.

Benefits of USB-C for Gaming Laptops:

- **Faster Data Transfer:** Ideal for transferring big files, such as game installations or videos.
- **Display Output:** USB-C can support video output to external monitors, allowing you to extend your display for dual-monitor sets or connect to ultra-high-definition displays.
- **Versatility:** With adapters, USB-C can handle HDMI, DisplayPort, and Ethernet connections, making it a highly adaptable port.

2. HDMI (High-Definition Multimedia Interface):

HDMI ports are important for connecting your laptop to an external monitor, TV, or projector. For gaming laptops, HDMI 2.0 or HDMI 2.1 are commonly found, giving high-bandwidth capabilities for 4K resolution at 60Hz (HDMI 2.0) or 120Hz (HDMI 2.1) refresh rates. If you're gaming on an external display, having an HDMI port ensures you can connect to bigger screens with ease.

Benefits of HDMI for Gaming Laptops:

- *External Display Compatibility:* HDMI allows you to connect to big external displays, monitors, or TVs.

- *VR and Multi-Display Setups:* For virtual reality (VR) gaming or dual-screen gaming setups, HDMI ports are important for connecting VR headsets or extra monitors.

- *Better Visual Experience:* HDMI allows high-definition video and audio output, allowing you to enjoy superior graphics and surround sound when connected to external monitors or TVs.

3. Thunderbolt 3/4:

Thunderbolt 3 and Thunderbolt 4 are high-speed ports that combine USB-C features with even greater data transfer speeds (up to 40Gbps). These ports allow for lightning-fast file transfers, high-resolution video output (including support for multiple 4K screens), and quick device charging. Thunderbolt also supports external GPU (eGPU) enclosures, which can improve your gaming laptop's graphics performance when connected to more powerful desktop GPUs.

Benefits of Thunderbolt for Gaming Laptops:

- ***Ultra-Fast Data Transfer:*** Useful for quickly transferring big files, running high-speed storage devices, or backing up game files.
- ***External GPU Support:*** Thunderbolt allows for external GPU setups, which is a great

choice for boosting your laptop's graphical performance.

- ***Multiple Monitors and High-Resolution Video:*** Thunderbolt allows daisy-chaining multiple devices, including external displays, ensuring a smooth multi-monitor experience.

4. Ethernet Port:

While Wi-Fi is often enough for most gamers, Ethernet (or RJ45) ports are important for those who value stable and low-latency online gaming. Wired connections usually provide a more consistent internet speed and lower latency compared to wireless connections, which is important in competitive gaming.

Benefits of Ethernet for Gaming Laptops:

- ***Stable, High-Speed Internet:*** A direct wired connection provides more reliable and faster internet speeds, which is especially useful for online gaming.

- **_Lower Latency:_** Wired connections reduce the risk of lag spikes and packet loss, giving a better overall gaming experience.

5. Other Ports (USB-A, Audio Jacks, etc.):

In addition to the modern ports listed above, you'll likely find a mix of USB-A ports for peripherals, audio jacks for headphones and microphones, and SD card readers for content creators who need quick access to photos or video files. These ports, while more common, are still important for completing the laptop's connectivity choices.

Benefits of These Additional Ports:

- **_USB-A Ports:_** Compatible with a wide range of peripherals like game mice, keyboards, and controllers.
- **_Audio Jacks:_** Essential for connecting headsets or external microphones for streaming or gaming contact.

SD Card Reader: Helpful for content makers who work with high-resolution images or video files, allowing for easy data transfer.

How to Choose the Right Ports for Your Needs

a). Casual gamers who don't need many external links can often do without Thunderbolt or multiple USB-C ports.

b). Competitive esports players may want to favor Ethernet ports for low-latency internet and HDMI/USB-C for multi-monitor setups.

c). Content producers will benefit from Thunderbolt and USB-C for fast file transfers and HDMI or DisplayPort for high-resolution external displays.

Cooling Solutions: Why Laptop Cooling is Crucial

When gaming on a high-performance laptop, cooling becomes a major concern. Gaming laptops tend to create a lot of heat due to the powerful components inside—especially the GPU and CPU. Without proper cooling, these components can overheat, leading to thermal throttling, which lowers performance, or worse, long-term damage to internal components.

That's why cooling solutions are critical when choosing a gaming laptop.

How Cooling Affects Gaming Performance

1. Thermal Throttling:

Thermal throttling happens when a laptop's cooling system can't keep up with the heat created by the CPU and GPU. In this case, the system instantly slows down its performance to prevent overheating. This can be especially noticeable during long gaming sessions or when running demanding games, as the frame rate may suddenly drop or gameplay may become choppy.

- **How to Avoid It:** Choosing a gaming laptop with an efficient cooling system, including multiple fans, heat pipes, or even vapor chamber cooling, helps avoid thermal throttling, ensuring consistent performance.

2. Noise Levels:

Cooling fans work hard to keep temperatures low, but they can also make a significant amount of noise. Laptops with aggressive cooling systems may become quite loud, especially during heavy games. For some users, this might be a distraction, especially in quieter settings.

- **How to Choose the Right Cooling Solution:** Look for laptops that strike a mix between cooling efficiency and fan noise. Many high-end gaming laptops feature "quiet mode" settings that can reduce fan noise while still keeping decent cooling.

3. Heat Management:

Good cooling solutions ensure that the heat is distributed efficiently across the laptop's chassis, avoiding hotspots that can cause discomfort or potential damage. Laptops with metal chassis (aluminum or magnesium alloy) often work better in heat control than plastic ones, as they dissipate heat more effectively.

External Cooling Pads: Worth the Investment?

For gamers who want to extend their laptop's lifespan and improve performance, external cooling pads can provide extra airflow and help keep temperatures in check. Cooling pads are especially useful for laptops with less robust built-in cooling systems.

1. Benefits of External Cooling Pads:

- **Improved Airflow:** Cooling pads help direct more air into the laptop's cooling vents, reducing the total temperature.
- **Portability:** Cooling pads are lightweight and portable, making them an easy accessory for games on the go.
- **Reduced Overheating:** Keeping the internal temperatures low can reduce the risk of thermal throttling and improve total performance.

2. When Are They Needed?

- **High-Performance Laptops:** If you're gaming on a laptop with powerful GPUs like the RTX 3080 or RTX 4090, external cooling pads can avoid overheating during extended sessions.
- **Laptops with Inefficient Cooling:** If your laptop tends to get hot under load and

experiences thermal throttling, a cooling pad might be a good buy.

3. Downsides of Cooling Pads:

- ***Increased size:*** Cooling pads add extra size to your setup, making the laptop less portable.
- ***Additional Power Draw:*** Cooling pads usually require additional power to operate, which can be an issue if you're gaming on battery.

Final Thoughts on Cooling Solutions

For the best experience, choose a gaming laptop with an efficient built-in cooling system, such as dual fans, heat pipes, or vapor chamber technology. If you're going to push your laptop to its limits, investing in a quality cooling pad could help improve performance and reduce heat. Always check reviews to see how well a laptop manages heat and maintains performance under load before making your choice.

By carefully considering these factors, you can ensure that your gaming laptop not only works well but also provides the necessary features and longevity for extended gaming and multitasking sessions.

Upgradability: Can You Upgrade Your Gaming Laptop?

One of the most important elements to consider when purchasing a gaming laptop is upgradability. Unlike desktop PCs, gaming laptops have limited upgrade choices due to their compact nature. However, some laptops allow for certain upgrades, which can extend their useful lifespan and improve speed as your gaming needs change.

What You Can Upgrade and How to Do It

1. RAM (Memory)

The most frequent upgrade option for gaming laptops is RAM. While many gaming laptops come with 8GB or 16GB of RAM, you can usually upgrade to 32GB if your laptop allows it. This upgrade is particularly useful if you're running memory-heavy apps alongside gaming, such as streaming software or video editing programs.

How to Upgrade:

- Check your laptop's manual or specs to see if it has an available RAM slot or if the current RAM is soldered to the motherboard.
- Purchase compatible RAM modules (same generation, speed, and size) and install them in the open slot or replace the current ones.
- Make sure to turn off the laptop, disconnect the battery (if possible), and follow static-free methods when handling the components.

2. Storage (SSD or HDD)

Upgrading your laptop's storage is another way to improve overall speed, especially when it comes to load times. Many gaming laptops come with a standard SSD (solid-state drive) for fast boot and game load times, but upgrading to a larger SSD or adding a second storage drive can provide more place for games, media, and files.

How to Upgrade:

- Check if your laptop has a second slot for an extra SSD or hard drive. If your laptop only has one slot, you can replace the current SSD with a larger one.
- For adding or changing an SSD, you will need to remove the back panel of your laptop, which can usually be done with a screwdriver.
- Install the new SSD, ensuring it's properly connected, and reinstall your operating system if replacing the main drive.

3. Battery

Upgrading or changing the battery can extend your laptop's portability. Over time, laptop batteries degrade, leading to lower battery life. Some gaming computers offer replaceable batteries, though many newer models feature built-in non-removable batteries.

How to Upgrade:

- If your laptop has a replaceable battery, you can find the compatible model from the maker and replace it yourself by removing the back panel.
- For non-removable batteries, you may need to send the laptop to a service center or authorized technician to change the battery.

4. Cooling System

Although not as popular as upgrading RAM or storage, some gaming laptops allow for improvements in the cooling system. You can change or upgrade cooling pads, add more thermal paste to the CPU/GPU, or use external cooling devices.

However, most internal cooling systems are set during production and aren't easily upgradeable.

How to Upgrade:

- Apply thermal paste if you want to improve the heat flow between the CPU/GPU and the cooling system.
- Use external cooling pads to reduce temperatures during intense gaming sessions and help your laptop keep high performance without overheating.

Limitations of Upgrading Gaming Laptops

While laptops offer some upgradability, their potential for future enhancements is restricted compared to desktops. GPUs are generally non-upgradable in gaming laptops, which means that if you want to upgrade your graphics performance significantly, you'll likely need to invest in a new laptop. Additionally, some high-end laptops use soldered RAM, blocking any future upgrades to memory.

In conclusion, while gaming laptops offer limited upgrade choices, you can still enhance your system's performance by upgrading RAM, storage, and possibly the battery or cooling systems. Always check the manufacturer's specs and ensure you're comfortable with DIY upgrades before diving in.

Operating System: Windows vs. Linux for Gaming

The operating system (OS) you choose for your gaming laptop can affect performance, compatibility, and general user experience. The two most popular OS choices for gaming are Windows and Linux, each with its own set of advantages and drawbacks. Understanding how each operating system affects gaming will help you make an informed choice based on your gaming and general computing needs.

Pros and Cons of Different OS Options for Gaming Laptops

1. Windows:

Windows 10 (and now Windows 11) is the most widely used operating system for gaming laptops. It offers broad compatibility with nearly all PC games, making it the go-to choice for gamers.

Pros of Windows:

a). Game Compatibility: Windows supports nearly all major game titles, including AAA games, indie games, and even older titles. Most games are optimized for Windows, ensuring maximum speed and stability.

b). Driver Support: Windows gives comprehensive support for hardware drivers, including those for GPUs, making it easy to update and optimize performance.

c). DirectX: DirectX is a set of multimedia APIs that improve gaming performance. Windows users have access to the latest versions of DirectX, which provide advanced graphics, better frame rates, and lower latency in games.

d). Game Store Integration: Windows supports major game stores like Steam, Epic Games Store, Origin, and Microsoft Store, giving access to a vast library of games.

e). Wide Hardware Support: All gaming laptops, including custom-built models, are created with Windows in mind. Windows OS offers compatibility with the widest range of peripherals, including gaming mice, controllers, and VR headsets.

Cons of Windows:

a). Bloatware: Some gaming laptops come pre-installed with unnecessary software and utilities that can affect speed or take up storage.

b). Cost: Windows licenses come at an extra cost (though many gaming laptops already come with Windows pre-installed).

c). System Updates: Windows often forces updates, which can sometimes interrupt your game experience or cause system instability.

2. Linux:

Linux, while not as popular as Windows for gaming, has made significant strides in recent years, thanks in part to efforts like Steam's Proton compatibility layer, which allows Windows games to run on Linux. Many gamers prefer Linux for its open-source nature, minimalistic design, and speed efficiency.

Pros of Linux:

a). Free and Open-Source: Unlike Windows, Linux is free to use. It's also highly customizable, making it ideal for users who want full control over their system's speed and interface.

b). Performance Efficiency: Linux tends to be more lightweight than Windows, which can result in better overall system performance, especially on lower-end hardware.

c). Less Bloatware: Linux distributions come without pre-installed software, so you can have a clean, efficient machine dedicated to gaming.

d). Proton and Wine: Tools like Proton (via Steam) and Wine allow Windows games to be played on Linux systems, greatly improving compatibility for gamers who want to use Linux.

Cons of Linux:

a). Limited Game Compatibility: While Linux is making strides in gaming, it still doesn't offer full support for all games. Many AAA titles may not run as smoothly as they do on Windows, and you may need to rely on workarounds (like Proton) to play certain games.

b). Driver Issues: While Linux has broad hardware support, it can sometimes struggle with the latest hardware drivers, especially for graphics cards. This can affect speed, especially with cutting-edge GPUs.

c). Lack of Game-Specific Features: Certain gaming peripherals and software features are not always available on Linux. Things like game overlays, performance monitoring tools, and even some specialized controllers may not work as smoothly as they do on Windows.

Which OS Should You Choose for Gaming?

Windows is the best choice for most gamers due to its compatibility with the biggest range of games, peripherals, and gaming software. It's the industry standard for gaming and ensures you get the most out of your game laptop.

Linux can be a good choice if you are a tech-savvy user who enjoys experimenting and customizing their gaming setup. It's also a great choice for those who value performance efficiency and want to avoid Windows' bloatware, but be aware of the limited game compatibility and driver problems.

For gamers who want simplicity, a wide range of game support, and ease of use, Windows is the clear choice. However, for those who are interested in an open-source system with the ability to tweak and customize, Linux may be worth considering—just be aware of the possible limitations when it comes to gaming.

Chapter 7: Troubleshooting and Maintaining Your Gaming Laptop

When you invest in a gaming laptop, you want to ensure that it performs well for years to come. However, like any high-performance machine, gaming laptops are prone to certain issues over time, especially if they are frequently used for demanding jobs like gaming, streaming, or content creation.

In this chapter, we will walk through common problems gamers face with their laptops and offer practical answers. Additionally, we'll cover tips on maintaining your laptop's performance over time to keep it running smoothly for as long as possible.

Common Issues in Gaming Laptops and How to Fix Them

Gaming laptops are complex machines with powerful components, which makes them vulnerable to a variety of issues. The most common problems often involve overheating and performance lag, both of which can seriously affect gaming and general laptop usage.

Overheating Problems and Solutions

Overheating is one of the most common problems in gaming laptops. These machines create a lot of heat, especially when running resource-heavy applications or playing graphically intense games. If your laptop overheats, it can lead to thermal throttling, where the CPU or GPU reduces its performance to prevent damage, or even cause lasting hardware damage if not addressed.

Here's how to spot and fix overheating issues:

1. Signs of Overheating:

- Fans running constantly or at high speeds.
- Laptop becoming hot to the touch, especially near the CPU or GPU area.
- Frequent system crashes or freezing during game sessions.
- Significant frame rate drops (thermal throttling) during games.

2. Solutions to Overheating:

a). Clean the Fans and Vents: Dust buildup inside the laptop can clog the cooling system, lowering airflow and causing higher temperatures. Regularly clean the fans and cooling vents using compressed air. Make sure to do this every few months to keep optimal airflow.

b). Use an External Cooling Pad: An external cooling pad can help provide extra airflow and lower the temperature of your laptop during long gaming sessions. Cooling pads are available with built-in fans that can direct airflow into the laptop's vents, helping to lower internal temperatures.

c). Apply New Thermal Paste: Over time, the thermal paste that sits between your CPU/GPU and the heatsink can dry out, reducing its usefulness in dissipating heat. If you're okay with disassembling your laptop, reapplying thermal paste can help improve heat transfer and lower temperatures.

d). Elevate the Laptop: Simply raising the back of the laptop to allow more air to flow underneath can make a major difference in cooling. Many external cooling pads come with built-in stands to help raise the laptop.

3. Advanced Solutions:

a). update the Cooling System: Some gaming laptops allow you to update the internal cooling system. This might mean adding an extra fan or replacing a fan with a more powerful one. Consult your laptop's manual or a professional technician to see if this is a choice for your model.

b). Undervolting the CPU/GPU: Undervolting includes reducing the voltage supplied to the CPU or GPU, which can help lower the temperature without sacrificing too much performance. This can be done using tools like Intel's XTU (Extreme Tuning Utility) or ThrottleStop for Intel processors. It's a bit technical, so it's recommended to read guides or seek professional help if you're new to this process.

Performance Lag and Fixes

Performance lag in gaming laptops is often caused by several factors, including insufficient system resources, bad optimization, or software issues. It can lead to lower frame rates, stuttering, and general sluggish performance while gaming or multitasking. Here are some common reasons of performance lag and how to fix them:

1. Causes of Performance Lag:

a). Overloaded RAM: If your system runs out of usable RAM, it can lead to lag, as the laptop starts swapping data between the RAM and slower storage.

b). CPU Overload: Running multiple resource-intensive apps (like a game, streaming software, and a web browser) can overload the CPU, leading to performance drops.

c). Outdated Drivers: Having outdated GPU, CPU, or peripheral drivers can cause compatibility problems and degrade efficiency.

d). Background Processes: Background processes like automatic updates, malware scans, or unnecessary software can consume important resources and cause lag.

2. Solutions to Fix Performance Lag:

a). Close Unnecessary Background Programs: Before gaming, close any non-essential apps running in the background. You can use the Task Manager (press Ctrl + Shift + Esc) to view and end jobs that are consuming resources.

b). Upgrade Your RAM: If your laptop only has 8GB of RAM, upgrading to 16GB or 32GB can greatly improve speed, especially for gaming and multitasking. Check if your laptop has available slots for extra RAM or if it's upgradable at all.

c). Update Your Drivers: Ensure that all system drivers, especially for your GPU and CPU, are up to date. Manufacturers often release driver updates that improve speed and fix bugs. You can update drivers through Device Manager or download them directly from the manufacturer's website (e.g., NVIDIA or AMD for GPU changes).

e). Clean and Optimize the System: Use built-in tools like Disk Cleanup and third-party software like CCleaner to remove useless files, clear out caches, and optimize the system. Running a disk defragmentation process (for HDDs) can also help speed up file entry times.

f). Check for Malware or Viruses: Malware and viruses can seriously slow down your laptop by consuming resources. Perform a full system check using antivirus software like Windows Defender or Malwarebytes to ensure your system is clean.

3. Advanced Solutions:

a). Reinstall the Operating System: If your laptop is running sluggish despite troubleshooting, reinstalling the operating system can remove bloatware and fix any problems with system files that might be causing lag.

b). Adjust Power Settings: In some cases, your laptop may be using power-saving settings that limit

CPU or GPU speed to save battery. Switch to High Performance mode in Power Options to ensure that your system is running at full ability when plugged in.

c). Upgrade Storage to SSD: If your laptop has a traditional HDD, upgrading to a Solid-State Drive (SSD) will greatly improve loading times, reduce lag, and boost overall system performance.

How to Maintain Your Laptop's Performance Over Time

To ensure your gaming laptop stays in top shape for years to come, regular maintenance is crucial. Proper maintenance helps avoid common issues like overheating, lag, and reduced battery life. Here are some important tips to keep your laptop running smoothly:

1. Regular Cleaning:

a). Internal Cleaning: Periodically clean the laptop's internal components, especially the fans and vents, using compressed air. This avoids dust buildup, which can block airflow and cause overheating.

b). External Cleaning: Wipe down the keyboard, screen, and exterior with a microfiber cloth to clear dirt and fingerprints. Keep your laptop in a clean, dust-free setting when possible.

2. Keep Software Up to Date:

a). System and Driver Updates: Regularly check for Windows updates and driver updates (especially for your GPU) to keep your system running at peak speed. Enable regular updates to ensure you don't miss important patches.

b). Gaming Platform Updates: Ensure that your Steam, Epic Games Store, or other gaming platforms are up to date, as they often release updates that improve speed and fix bugs in games.

3. Manage Storage Efficiently:

a). Avoid Running Out of Space: Ensure that you don't fill up your hard drive, especially your SSD. If your SSD is getting close to full, consider offloading non-essential files to an external hard drive or cloud storage to keep the system going efficiently.

b). Uninstall Unused Programs: Regularly review and remove programs that you no longer use to free up room and reduce clutter.

4. Battery Care:

a). Avoid Overcharging: If your laptop stays plugged in for extended times, avoid charging it to 100% constantly, as this can degrade the battery over time. Aim to keep the battery between 20-80% for best health.

b). Use Battery Saver: For longer battery life during light usage, enable battery saver mode in the power settings to limit background processes and conserve power.

5. Temperature Monitoring:

Monitor CPU and GPU Temperatures: Use tools like HW Monitor or MSI Afterburner to keep an eye on your laptop's temperatures, especially during gaming sessions. If you find temperatures exceeding 85°C, it may be time to clean the laptop's internal components or consider additional cooling measures.

Cleaning, Dusting, and Proper Storage

Keeping your gaming laptop clean and well-maintained is vital for its longevity and best performance. Dust, dirt, and grime can collect both inside and outside your laptop, causing performance degradation, overheating, and even permanent damage if not addressed regularly. Here's how to keep your game laptop in top condition:

1. Internal Cleaning:

a). Dusting the Vents and Fans: The internal cooling system is often the first area affected by dust buildup. Over time, dust can clog the vents and fans, lowering airflow and causing overheating. Use compressed air to blow out dust from the vents and fans, but make sure to do this carefully to avoid damaging sensitive components. It's recommended to clean the internals every few months, especially if you notice the laptop running hot or if it's been used in a dusty environment.

b). Thermal Paste Reapplication: If you're okay opening up your laptop, reapplying thermal paste between the CPU/GPU and heatsinks can improve heat dissipation. Over time, the thermal paste can dry out, leading to poor heat transfer and higher temperatures. This can help lower the risk of overheating during long gaming sessions.

2. External Cleaning:

a). Keyboard and Screen: The keyboard and screen are often the most visible parts of your laptop. Use a microfiber cloth to wipe down the screen and keyboard regularly to clear fingerprints, dust, and smudges. Avoid using harsh chemicals that could hurt the surface.

b). Avoid Eating and Drinking Near Your Laptop: This may seem clear, but liquids and food particles can spill into the laptop's vents, causing damage or internal short circuits. Keep your gaming area clean and free from possible hazards to your laptop.

3. Proper Storage:

a). Storing Your Laptop: When you're not gaming, store your laptop in a cool, dry place to avoid dust buildup and heat damage. Avoid leaving it on soft surfaces like beds or chairs, as this can block the cooling vents and cause the laptop to overheat.

Ideally, store it on a hard surface where airflow is not blocked.

b). Carrying Your Laptop: If you travel often with your game laptop, invest in a protective carrying case to shield it from drops and scratches. Some cases come with extra compartments for accessories like chargers and external hard drives, keeping everything organized and safe.

Software Optimization and Updates

Keeping your system and software optimized ensures smooth and efficient operation of your gaming laptop, improving overall performance and reducing possible problems. Here's how you can keep optimal software performance:

1. Operating System Updates:

Regular updates to your Windows (or other OS) are important for maintaining security and performance. Microsoft makes updates that fix bugs, improve system stability, and provide new features. Always install critical updates and driver updates, especially for your GPU, CPU, and Wi-Fi drivers, as these can affect game performance and system responsiveness.

2. Game and Platform Updates:

Gaming platforms like Steam, Epic Games Store, or Origin regularly update both the platform itself and the games you own. Ensure that auto-updates are set for your games so you don't miss important patches or fixes that could affect gameplay. Keeping games up to date ensures compatibility with newer systems and stops crashes or bugs that could disrupt your gaming experience.

3. Optimize Startup Programs:

Excessive startup programs can slow down your system and affect game performance. Open Task Manager and review the list of apps that run when your system boots. Disable unnecessary programs from running at startup, leaving only those that are important for your gaming experience.

4. Disk Cleanup and Defragmentation:

Over time, your laptop's storage can become filled with junk files. Use the Disk Cleanup tool on Windows to remove temporary files, system files, and cache that could be slowing down your laptop. If you're using a traditional HDD, try running disk defragmentation to reorganize fragmented files for faster access. However, if you have an SSD, defragmentation is not necessary, but running TRIM operations can help keep it in optimal shape.

5. Antivirus Software:

Ensure that you have a good antivirus program loaded to protect your system from malware, viruses, and other malicious software. Regular scans help avoid any security threats that could compromise system performance. Make sure your antivirus software is up-to-date with the latest definitions to protect your laptop from new threats.

When to Repair vs. Replace Your Laptop

Gaming computers are an investment, but like any piece of technology, they have a limited lifespan. Over time, the speed may begin to degrade, and you might face challenges when running the latest games. Knowing when it's time to repair or replace your laptop can save you money and stress.

1. Signs That It Might Be Time to Repair:

a). Overheating Issues: If your laptop is frequently overheating, despite cleaning and improving airflow, it might be time to replace the cooling system or reapply thermal paste. Overheating can cause damage to internal components if not addressed, but a repair might serve to extend the laptop's life.

b). Performance Decline: If your laptop is still usable but is showing signs of performance lag, upgrading RAM or replacing your HDD with an SSD might help. Upgrading certain components can give your laptop a new start on life, especially for less demanding games.

c). Battery Problems: If your battery is no longer holding a charge or is draining too quickly, replacing the battery could be an easy fix. Many gaming laptops offer battery replacement choices.

2. Signs That It's Time to Replace:

a). Outdated Hardware: If your gaming laptop is struggling to keep up with current games, even after upgrading components like RAM or storage, it may be time to replace it. GPUs and CPUs cannot be upgraded in most gaming laptops, so if your system can no longer handle new titles, upgrading the whole system is often the best option.

b). High Repair Costs: If you're facing costly repairs (such as motherboard or GPU replacement), it may make more sense to buy a new laptop rather than continue putting money into repairs. This is especially true if your laptop is several years old and no longer under protection.

c). Frequent System Failures: If your laptop is constantly having system crashes, motherboard failures, or hard drive failures, it could indicate that the system is at the end of its life. At this point, replacing the laptop might be the most cost-effective choice.

How to Decide If It's Time to Upgrade Your Gaming Rig

1. Evaluate Gaming Needs:

The gaming industry evolves rapidly, with new games needing increasingly powerful hardware. If you find yourself constantly having to lower graphics settings or struggling to play the latest games, upgrading to a new laptop with more powerful components, like a better GPU, faster CPU, or higher refresh rate display, might be necessary.

2. Future-Proofing:

When upgrading, look for a laptop that can handle future game updates. A high-end GPU like the RTX 3080 or RTX 4090, along with a fast CPU and 32GB of RAM, will give you the freedom to enjoy games at ultra settings for years to come.

3. Consider Your Budget:

Gaming computers can be expensive, so consider how much you're willing to spend. Sometimes, upgrading your current laptop (e.g., adding more RAM, switching to an SSD, or replacing a worn-out battery) is sufficient for getting more life out of it without the need for a full replacement.

we've explored how to keep your laptop's performance through regular cleaning, software optimization, and knowing when to repair or replace your device. Keeping your gaming laptop in good shape not only ensures better performance over time but also helps you avoid costly repairs and downtime. By following the maintenance tips and troubleshooting steps in this chapter, you can extend the lifespan of your laptop and keep it running smoothly for years of enjoyable gaming.

Chapter 8: Gaming Laptop Accessories

When it comes to building the ultimate gaming setup, the gaming laptop itself is just one part of the equation. To truly elevate your gaming experience, the right accessories can make a big difference. From mice, keyboards, and headsets to external monitors, mousepads, and laptop stands, each accessory plays a key role in improving both comfort and performance during long game sessions.

In this chapter, we will discuss the important accessories for your gaming laptop, explore how to ensure they're compatible with your laptop, and give you tips on how to set everything up to get the most out of your gaming experience.

Essential Accessories for Your Gaming Laptop Setup

To get the best possible gaming experience, it's important to spend in the right accessories. These peripherals improve comfort, control, and performance during gameplay, helping you stay competitive and immerse yourself fully in your games.

Mice, Keyboards, and Headsets: Must-Have Gear

1. Gaming Mouse:

A gaming mouse is one of the most important accessories for any serious gamer. Unlike regular mice, gaming mice are designed with higher precision, faster reaction times, and better ergonomics to help improve your gameplay. Here's what to look for when picking a gaming mouse:

a) DPI (Dots Per Inch): This refers to the mouse's sensitivity. Higher DPI means the cursor will move faster across the screen, which is important for fast-paced games like first-person shooters (FPS). Many gaming mice feature adjustable DPI settings, allowing you to switch between different levels of sensitivity based on the game.

b) Ergonomics: Since players spend long hours playing, it's important to choose a mouse that's comfortable for extended use. Look for ergonomic shapes that reduce strain on your wrist and fingers.

c) Polling Rate: The polling rate controls how often the mouse sends data to the computer. A higher asking rate results in faster response times. Gaming mice usually have polling rates of 1000Hz or higher, which is ideal for quick actions in games.

d) Buttons and Customization: Extra buttons on the mouse allow you to bind specific actions, such as reloading, switching guns, or activating abilities, making gameplay more efficient.

Popular Options:

- Logitech G Pro X Superlight (highly suggested for esports players)
- Razer DeathAdder V2 (comfortable, ergonomic, and accurate) SteelSeries Rival 600 (offers dual sensors for improved accuracy)

2. Gaming Keyboard:

A gaming keyboard is important for both typing and controlling your character in games. These keyboards are intended to offer better performance with faster response times, customizable key mappings, and greater durability compared to standard keyboards.

a) Mechanical vs. Membrane Keyboards: Mechanical keyboards are more famous in the gaming community due to their faster response times and tactile feedback. They are highly durable and provide a more enjoyable typing experience. Membrane keyboards are quieter and more cheap, but they don't offer the same level of precision.

b) Key Switch Types: Mechanical keyboards come with different key switches (e.g., Cherry MX, Razer Optical). Each switch type has its own traits, such as tactile feedback, actuation force, and sound. Choose the type that fits your playstyle and typing preference.

c) RGB Lighting: Many game keyboards feature customizable RGB lighting, which can add an aesthetic touch to your setup. Some models allow you to program different colors for individual keys or give lighting effects based on in-game actions.

Popular Options:

- Corsair K95 RGB Platinum (premium build, great for FPS and MMO games)

- Razer Huntsman V2 Analog (featuring analog optical buttons)
- Logitech G Pro X (small design with swappable key switches)

3. Gaming Headset:

A good gaming headset is important for clear communication with teammates, immersing yourself in game audio, and getting that competitive edge. Look for headsets that provide high-quality sound, comfortable fit, and noise reduction to fully immerse yourself in your games.

a) *Sound Quality:* For immersive gameplay, you'll want a headset that offers surround sound or stereo sound. Many speakers come with 7.1 surround sound, which helps with directional audio, making it easier to hear footsteps, gunshots, and other in-game sounds.

b) *Microphone:* A noise-cancelling microphone is important for clear communication with teammates.

Look for a headset with a removable or adjustable microphone for better control.

c) Comfort: Since game sessions can last for hours, comfort is key. Look for headsets with padded ear cups and a flexible headband.

Popular Options:

- SteelSeries Arctis 7 (wireless, comfy, great sound quality)
- Razer Kraken V3 Pro (features THX spatial audio for better immersion) o Corsair HS70 Pro (solid, budget-friendly choice with good sound)

External Monitors, Mousepads, and Laptop Stands

1. External Monitors:

While gaming on a laptop is convenient, external monitors can improve your gaming experience, especially if you prefer larger displays or higher refresh rates. Look for monitors that allow higher refresh rates (e.g., 144Hz, 240Hz) and low input lag to ensure smooth gameplay.

a) Screen Size and Resolution: A bigger screen size (e.g., 27-inch or more) gives you more visual real estate, which can improve immersion. Higher resolutions like 1440p or 4K offer sharper visuals, but these require a more powerful laptop GPU to handle challenging games.

b). Refresh Rate: For competitive gaming, 144Hz or higher refresh rates are necessary. They provide smoother visuals and decrease motion blur during fast-paced games.

c). G-Sync/FreeSync: If your laptop's GPU allows it, look for monitors with NVIDIA G-Sync or AMD FreeSync, which reduce screen tearing and stuttering for a more fluid gaming experience.

Popular Options:

- ASUS ROG Swift PG259QN (360Hz, great for esports and fast-paced gaming)
- Dell S2721DGF (27-inch, QHD, 165Hz with FreeSync)
- LG 27GN950-B (4K screen, 144Hz refresh rate)

2. Mousepads:

A gaming mousepad can improve your mouse accuracy and comfort during play. Look for one that offers a smooth surface, non-slip base, and ample room for large mouse movements, especially for FPS games.

Popular Options:

- SteelSeries QcK (affordable, generally recommended by gamers)
- Logitech G640 (great mix of speed and control)
- Corsair MM300 (highly durable and great for larger mice)

3. Laptop Stands:

A laptop stand can elevate your laptop to a more ergonomic position, reducing neck and back strain during long game sessions. Many stands also provide extra cooling, as they increase airflow beneath the laptop.

Popular Options:

- Rain Design mStand (sleek, comfortable, highly durable)
- Cooler Master NotePal U3 (offers extra cooling with fans)

Peripheral Compatibility: Making Sure Everything Works Together

When adding accessories to your gaming setup, it's important to ensure that all your peripherals are compatible with your gaming laptop. Compatibility issues can cause frustrations, such as not being able to use certain features or having connectivity problems.

How to Ensure Your Laptop and Peripherals Are Fully Compatible

1. Check the Ports on Your Laptop:

Ensure your laptop has the necessary ports for connecting devices. For example, if you plan to use a wired mouse or keyboard, check if your laptop has enough USB-A or USB-C ports. If you want to connect an external monitor, make sure your laptop has an HDMI, USB-C, or DisplayPort connection, based on the monitor's input requirements.

2. Wireless vs. Wired:

Wireless peripherals (like wireless mice and headsets) are handy, but make sure your laptop has the needed wireless technologies like Bluetooth or a USB receiver for a seamless connection. o Wired peripherals require USB ports or specific display connections. Ensure your laptop has enough ports to handle multiple wired devices if needed.

3. Power Requirements:

Some high-end gaming accessories, like external monitors or external GPUs, may require extra power, which could be provided through USB-C (with Power Delivery) or a dedicated power adapter. Ensure that your laptop supports the necessary power delivery choices to handle these peripherals.

Connecting to External Displays and VR Gear

1. External Displays:

When connecting your gaming laptop to an external monitor, ensure that you select the right display output on your laptop. Use the proper HDMI, DisplayPort, or USB-C connections, depending on the monitor's requirements. Ensure that the resolution and refresh rate settings are adjusted properly in your laptop's display settings.

2. Virtual Reality (VR) Gear:

VR needs low-latency connections and powerful hardware. If you plan to connect your laptop to VR gear like the Oculus Rift or HTC Vive, check for the needed USB and HDMI/DisplayPort ports. Additionally, make sure your GPU and CPU meet the minimum requirements for a smooth VR experience.

In this chapter, we've covered the important accessories that can enhance your gaming laptop setup, including mice, keyboards, headsets, and more. We also covered the importance of ensuring peripheral compatibility and how to properly connect to external displays and VR gear for the ultimate gaming experience. By investing in the right accessories and making sure they're compatible with your laptop, you can take your game setup to the next level.

Chapter 9: Top Gaming Laptop Models in 2024

There are so many game laptops on the market that it can be hard to pick the right one. Every type of player can find a model that works for them, no matter how much money they have or how strong they need their laptop to be. You can read about the best cheap and mid-range gaming laptops for 2024 in this chapter. We will focus on the features, speed specs, and value for money that make each one stand out.

Top Budget Picks

In 2024, the budget gaming laptop market offers amazing performance at an affordable price point. These laptops are great for casual gamers or those looking to enjoy their favorite games without spending too much. While budget gaming laptops may not boast the high-end specifications of premium models, they still offer solid gaming experiences for 1080p gaming and casual gaming sessions.

Best Budget Gaming Laptops in 2024

1. Acer Nitro 5 (2024 Edition)

- CPU: Intel Core i5-11400H (or AMD Ryzen 5 5600H)
- GPU: NVIDIA GeForce GTX 1650 / GTX 1660 Ti
- RAM: 8GB (expandable to 32GB)
- Storage: 512GB SSD
- Display: 15.6-inch Full HD, 144Hz
- Price: ~$700 - $850

Pros:

- Strong gaming performance for the price, able to handle famous titles like Fortnite, Apex Legends, and Minecraft at medium settings.
- Solid build quality with good cooling performance, keeping temperatures under control during long sessions.
- High speed rate display (144Hz) for smooth gameplay, especially in fast-paced games.

Cons:

- 8GB of RAM is fine for most casual games but can be limiting for more demanding multitasking.
- The design is relatively bulky, making the laptop heavier than some options.
- Why It's Great for Budget Gamers: The Acer Nitro 5 is a good choice for gamers who want to enjoy modern games at a decent frame rate without breaking the bank. With its powerful

GPU options and high refresh rate monitor, it gives great value for money.

2. HP Pavilion Gaming Laptop (2024 Edition)

- CPU: AMD Ryzen 5 5600H
- GPU: NVIDIA GeForce GTX 1650
- RAM: 8GB
- Storage: 512GB SSD
- Display: 15.6-inch Full HD, 60Hz
- Price: ~$650 - $750

Pros:

- Affordable, giving decent performance for 1080p gaming with medium settings.
- Lightweight and portable design, great for gamers on the go.
- Good battery life for a gaming laptop, giving up to 8 hours of use on a single charge.

Cons:

- The 60Hz display limits the general gaming experience, especially in fast-paced action titles.
- Limited RAM expansion choices, making it harder to upgrade the system in the future.

Why It's Great for Budget Gamers: The HP Pavilion is a safe choice for gamers on a budget who still want a portable and well-built machine. While its refresh rate is lower, the general gaming experience is smooth, especially for less demanding titles.

3. Lenovo Legion 5 15

- CPU: AMD Ryzen 5 5600H
- GPU: NVIDIA GeForce GTX 1650
- RAM: 8GB (expandable to 16GB)
- Storage: 512GB SSD
- Display: 15.6-inch Full HD, 120Hz
- Price: ~$750

Pros:

- Offers a faster refresh rate (120Hz), which improves the gaming experience in fast-paced games.
- Solid build and good cooling system to keep performance during longer gaming sessions.
- Good value for money with decent performance and storage choices.

Cons:

- Battery life can be limited during heavy game sessions.
- 8GB of RAM might not be sufficient for future-proofing, especially for multitasking or running high-end games.

Why It's Great for Budget Gamers: The Lenovo Legion 5 hits a good balance between performance and price. It's equipped with a high refresh rate display and a strong GPU, making it ideal for casual gaming or entry-level competitive play.

Top Mid-Range Picks

As we move into the mid-range gaming laptop category, these machines offer significantly better performance and features compared to budget choices. Mid-range laptops are great for gamers who want higher settings, better frame rates, and smoother performance in more demanding games. In 2024, mid-range models provide excellent value for gamers who need something more powerful than a budget laptop without going into the high-end price band.

Best Mid-Range Gaming Laptops in 2024

1. ASUS ROG Strix G15 (2024 Edition)

- CPU: Intel Core i7-12700H
- GPU: NVIDIA GeForce RTX 3060
- RAM: 16GB
- Storage: 1TB SSD

- Display: 15.6-inch Full HD, 165Hz
- Price: ~$1,200

Pros:

- Excellent performance in AAA games at 1080p with ultra settings.
- High refresh rate (165Hz) and fast response time for smooth games.
- Great cooling system, ensuring good performance during extended sessions.
- 1TB SSD gives ample storage space for games and other files.

Cons:

- Battery life is somewhat limited when gaming actively.
- On the heavier side, making it less portable compared to ultra-thin gaming computers.

Why It's Great for Mid-Range Gamers: The ASUS ROG Strix G15 is a powerhouse in the mid-range category. It's perfect for gamers who want strong performance for modern AAA titles and esports games at higher settings, all while having great cooling and storage.

2. MSI GF65 Thin 10UE

- CPU: Intel Core i7-10750H
- GPU: NVIDIA GeForce RTX 3060
- RAM: 16GB
- Storage: 512GB SSD
- Display: 15.6-inch Full HD, 144Hz
- Price: ~$1,100

Pros:

- Lightweight and thin design makes it movable and easy to carry around.
- Powerful GPU for high settings and smooth 1080p games.
- 144Hz display offers smooth gameplay in fast-paced action games.

- Decent battery life for gaming computers in this range.

Cons:

- The 512GB SSD might be limiting for users with big game libraries or media files.
- Not as visually stunning as some competitors, but useful for the price.

Why It's Great for Mid-Range Gamers: The MSI GF65 Thin is an excellent choice for gamers who need powerful performance in a small and portable package. With RTX 3060 graphics and a 144Hz display, this laptop is great for smooth gameplay in competitive and AAA games.

3. Razer Blade 15 Base Model (2024 Edition)

- CPU: Intel Core i7-12700H
- GPU: NVIDIA GeForce RTX 3060
- RAM: 16GB
- Storage: 512GB SSD

- Display: 15.6-inch Full HD, 144Hz
- Price: ~$1,500

Pros:

- Sleek, luxury design with an ultra-thin chassis.
- Great performance for AAA and esports games with RTX 3060.
- Excellent build quality with a solid metal body.
- Good battery life for a game laptop, lasting up to 6-8 hours under light usage.

Cons:

- Higher price compared to other mid-range computers with similar specs.
- The 512GB SSD might be too small for people who store a lot of games or media files.

Why It's Great for Mid-Range Gamers: The Razer Blade 15 offers a great gaming experience with powerful hardware, a fantastic display, and a thin design. It's great for gamers who want a blend of style, portability, and performance.

Top Premium Picks

High-end gaming laptops are the ultimate choice for gamers who expect exceptional performance, reliability, and immersive features. These laptops can handle the most graphically intense games, provide higher resolutions, and offer faster refresh rates, all while providing an uncompromising gaming experience. If you're looking for the best of the best, these are the top premium game laptops for 2024.

Best High-End Gaming Laptops in 2024

1. Alienware x17 R2

- CPU: Intel Core i9-12900HK
- GPU: NVIDIA GeForce RTX 3080 Ti
- RAM: 32GB
- Storage: 1TB SSD

- Display: 17.3-inch 4K, 120Hz
- Price: ~$2,100 - $2,500

Pros:

- Powered by Intel's latest 12th Gen i9 and the RTX 3080 Ti, providing fantastic performance for AAA games and VR.
- Stunning 4K display with excellent color accuracy, perfect for immersive games and content creation.
- Advanced cooling system to manage intense game sessions, ensuring no thermal throttling.
- 16-hour battery life under light usage, and good power management for gaming on the go.

Cons:

- Very expensive compared to other high-end types.
- Large, heavy form, not ideal for ultra-portability.

Why It's Great for Premium Gamers: The Alienware x17 R2 is a powerhouse with exceptional graphical skills and an immersive display. It's ideal for gamers who want high-end performance for both gaming and multimedia jobs, with a gorgeous 4K screen and top-tier cooling for long sessions.

2. Razer Blade 17 (2024 Edition)

- CPU: Intel Core i9-12900H
- GPU: NVIDIA GeForce RTX 3080 Ti
- RAM: 32GB
- Storage: 1TB SSD
- Display: 17.3-inch QHD, 165Hz
- Price: ~$2,200

Pros:

- Ultra-slim and sleek design with premium build quality, giving both portability and performance.

- 165Hz QHD display for smooth visuals, ideal for both competitive games and cinematic experiences.
- Top-tier performance in all aspects, including great multitasking for gaming, video editing, and more.
- High-quality mechanical keyboard with Razer's custom RGB Chroma lights.

Cons:

- High price point, making it out of reach for budget-conscious players.
- Some users may find the big screen size (17.3 inches) too bulky for portability.

Why It's Great for Premium Gamers: The Razer Blade 17 offers the perfect mix of power, portability, and premium build quality. It's an ideal choice for gamers who prioritize having the best visual experience and high-end gaming performance without sacrificing portability.

3. MSI GE76 Raider

- CPU: Intel Core i9-12900HK
- GPU: NVIDIA GeForce RTX 3080 Ti
- RAM: 32GB
- Storage: 1TB SSD
- Display: 17.3-inch 4K, 120Hz
- Price: ~$2,500

Pros:

- Offers excellent performance for 4K gaming and content creation, with the RTX 3080 Ti easily powering challenging games at ultra settings.
- High-quality 4K display with vibrant colors and high contrast, great for immersive gaming.
- Great cooling performance, ensuring that the laptop stays cool under heavy use.

Cons:

- Very big and heavy, not ideal for portability.

- Premium price, but justified by the strong specs and features.

Why It's Great for Premium Gamers: The MSI GE76 Raider is built for gamers who expect the best in performance, screen quality, and cooling. It's ideal for 4K gaming and offers superior specs that can handle demanding AAA games, esports, and content creation with ease.

VR-Ready and Esports Laptops

With the rise of virtual reality (VR) and esports, certain gaming laptops have been built to handle the demanding requirements of both. These computers feature powerful GPUs, low latency, and high refresh rates, making them ideal for competitive gaming and VR experiences that require immersive and responsive games.

The Best Laptops for Competitive and Virtual Reality Gaming

1. ASUS ROG Zephyrus G14 (2024 Edition)

- CPU: AMD Ryzen 9 7940HS
- GPU: NVIDIA GeForce RTX 4070
- RAM: 16GB
- Storage: 1TB SSD
- Display: 14-inch QHD, 120Hz
- Price: ~$1,700

Pros:

- Compact yet powerful, with RTX 4070 graphics that provide smooth VR performance and high settings for competitive games.
- Excellent QHD display with a 120Hz refresh rate, great for esports and fast-paced games.
- Lightweight and portable design, great for VR games on the go.
- Advanced cooling system to control heat during long gaming sessions.

Cons:

- Smaller display (14-inch), which may not be ideal
- for users who prefer bigger screens.
- Expensive for a laptop with a relatively smaller screen size.

Why It's Great for VR and Esports: The ASUS ROG Zephyrus G14 offers exceptional portability without compromising on strength. It's great for esports players who need a laptop that can handle high FPS in competitive games and provide a solid VR experience.

2. HP Omen 17

- CPU: Intel Core i9-12900H
- GPU: NVIDIA GeForce RTX 3080
- RAM: 32GB
- Storage: 1TB SSD
- Display: 17.3-inch Full HD, 144Hz
- Price: ~$2,000

Pros:

- RTX 3080 GPU promises great performance for both VR and esports games, with smooth gameplay even at ultra settings.
- The 144Hz display offers a smooth and responsive experience, perfect for competitive gaming.
- Excellent cooling system that keeps the laptop at optimal temperatures during intense games and VR sessions.

Cons:

- Heavier than some other game laptops, which can limit portability.
- The 17.3-inch screen size can be too large for gamers wanting a more portable solution.

Why It's Great for VR and Esports: The HP Omen 17 is a top-tier choice for gamers who expect the best performance for esports and VR gaming. Its

RTX 3080 and high-refresh-rate display make it great for competitive and immersive gaming.

3. Lenovo Legion 7i

- CPU: Intel Core i9-12900HK
- GPU: NVIDIA GeForce RTX 3080
- RAM: 32GB
- Storage: 1TB SSD
- Display: 15.6-inch Full HD, 165Hz
- Price: ~$2,000

Pros:

- The RTX 3080 and Intel Core i9 provide exceptional VR performance and frame rates for competitive games.
- 165Hz display provides smooth visuals for high-speed esports games.
- Excellent build quality and durability for both games and portability.

Cons:

- Relatively heavy compared to some ultra-thin computers.
- The Full HD display is great, but some may prefer a higher resolution for more immersive games.

Why It's Great for VR and Esports: The Lenovo Legion 7i is designed with esports and VR gamers in mind, giving top-tier performance in both fields. It's the perfect laptop for those who need a machine that can handle both competitive games and immersive virtual reality experiences.

These models represent the pinnacle of performance, giving incredible graphics, smooth gameplay, and stunning displays to improve your overall gaming experience. Whether you're a professional player or an enthusiast looking to explore the world of VR, these premium laptops provide everything you need for an immersive, high-performance experience.

Chapter 10: Future Trends in Gaming Laptops (Detailed Version)

The gaming laptop market is experiencing significant transformations, with rapid advancements in hardware, connectivity, and software. As we move into 2024 and beyond, gaming computers are set to become more powerful, versatile, and tailored to new technologies. From the integration of AI and 5G connectivity to the rise of cloud gaming, future gaming laptops will change the way we play games, both now and in the future.

In this chapter, we will explore these emerging trends in depth, examining how they will impact gaming laptops and how they will continue to meet the needs of both casual gamers and professionals.

What's Next for Gaming Laptop Technology?

Gaming laptops are evolving beyond their traditional limits, incorporating innovations that improve performance, connectivity, and user experience. Let's look at some of the most exciting advances in gaming laptop technology that will define the future of the market:

1. AI-Powered Laptops

Artificial intelligence (AI) is set to revolutionize how gaming laptops perform and adapt to user needs. AI will not only boost gameplay but also improve system efficiency and personalization. Here's how AI will impact gaming computers in the near future:

a) Performance Optimization: AI can dynamically change system resources in real-time to ensure the best performance. For example, AI-powered systems will monitor the temperature of the

CPU, GPU, and RAM during game sessions, adjusting the fan speeds or shifting processing loads to reduce heat buildup.

The AI will also optimize power usage, ensuring that your laptop runs at peak speed when needed and conserves energy during light usage. This will minimize thermal throttling, which often happens in high-performance laptops under heavy loads, thereby keeping consistent frame rates during long gaming sessions.

b) *AI-Assisted Game Performance:* AI can analyze gameplay in real time and automatically change graphics settings based on the game's requirements and the laptop's capabilities. For example, AI can intelligently change visual effects like shadows, anti-aliasing, and textures based on available GPU power, ensuring smooth performance while maximizing visual fidelity. This removes the need for manual adjustments and offers a seamless experience, especially for gamers who aren't as tech-savvy.

c) Personalized Gaming Experience: Future gaming laptops will use AI to learn your gaming habits, tastes, and playstyles. Over time, the system will change gameplay settings, lighting, sound, and even suggest new games based on your preferences. AI will also provide personalized suggestions for game performance tweaks, helping you get the most out of your laptop's hardware.

d) ***Why It's Important:*** AI integration will help gaming computers to become smarter and more intuitive. By optimizing performance and giving personalized settings, AI will ensure that you get the best possible gaming experience without needing to constantly tweak settings or worry about performance issues.

2. 5G Connectivity for Faster Gaming

The next frontier in internet connectivity, 5G, will have a profound impact on how gaming laptops work, especially in terms of cloud gaming and online multiplayer experiences. As 5G networks continue to roll out, they will allow much faster, more stable connections that will be crucial for gaming.

a) Ultra-Low Latency for Online Gaming: One of the most important benefits of 5G technology is its ability to provide ultra-low latency—reducing the delay between a player's action and the result on screen. This is particularly important for competitive games, where every millisecond counts. In games such as Fortnite, Apex Legends, or Call of Duty, low delay can mean the difference between winning and losing. With 5G, players will experience virtually no lag or delay, ensuring smoother gameplay and more responsive controls.

b) Faster Downloads and Streaming: 5G will greatly improve download speeds, allowing you to access new games, updates, and patches in a fraction of the time. Additionally, the enhanced bandwidth offered by 5G will allow seamless game streaming in high definition, including 4K or even 8K resolution. Gamers will no longer have to wait for long downloads or worry about their internet link buffering during a stream.

c) Mobile Gaming: The introduction of 5G will also allow mobile gaming to reach new heights. Laptops with built-in 5G connectivity will allow you to game on the go, even in remote places with limited access to Wi-Fi. This opens up new opportunities for portable, high-performance gaming that can be done anywhere.

Why It's Important: 5G will reduce latency, increase download speeds, and enhance game streaming, ensuring that gaming laptops can offer better online experiences and support cloud-based gaming without compromising performance.

The Future of Gaming Laptop Design

As speed continues to improve, gaming laptops are becoming more versatile, thinner, and lighter without sacrificing power. The goal is on creating designs that are not only more powerful but also easier to carry and more comfortable to use. Here's what the future holds in terms of game laptop design:

1. Lighter, Thinner, More Powerful

Gaming laptops have usually been bulky and heavy due to their powerful hardware and extensive cooling systems. However, as GPU and CPU technology continues to evolve, manufacturers are focused on reducing size and weight without compromising performance.

a). Compact Power: The latest advancements in laptop cooling and the creation of more efficient components will allow gaming laptops to pack powerful hardware into thinner, more portable designs. GPUs like NVIDIA's RTX 4000 series and AMD's RDNA 3 will continue to push the limits of performance, while smaller, more efficient CPUs will ensure that gaming laptops can offer desktop-level performance in a portable form factor.

b). Smarter Cooling Solutions: To fit the powerful hardware in slim designs, future gaming laptops will feature advanced cooling solutions such as liquid metal cooling, vapor chambers, and dynamic cooling systems that adjust airflow in real-time to match the laptop's performance needs. These cooling solutions will prevent overheating while ensuring that the laptop remains slim and sleek.

c). More Premium Materials: Gaming laptops will increasingly use premium materials such as magnesium alloy, carbon fiber, and aluminum to reduce weight while keeping durability. These materials not only make computers lighter but also provide a more attractive finish and better heat dissipation.

Why It's Important: The future of gaming laptop design will combine portability and power, giving gamers the freedom to play their favorite games anywhere without carrying around a bulky machine.

How Cloud Gaming Will Affect Gaming Laptops

Cloud gaming is one of the most exciting developments in the gaming business. With services like NVIDIA GeForce Now, Xbox Cloud Gaming, and Google Stadia, gamers can now play high-end games without having powerful local hardware. Instead, games are rendered on remote servers and streamed straight to the user's device. So, how will this change affect gaming laptops?

1. Will We Still Need Powerful Gaming Laptops?

As cloud gaming becomes more common, the need for high-end local hardware may decrease. In theory, cloud gaming could allow you to play graphically demanding games on a mid-range or even budget laptop as long as you have a stable, high-speed internet link. However, there are still several reasons why powerful gaming laptops will continue to be important.

a) Local Performance vs. Streaming: While cloud gaming removes the need for powerful hardware, there are still limitations. High-speed internet connections are important, and the quality of your gaming experience depends on the stability of your connection. For competitive players, low-latency connections and high frame rates may be important, and even with cloud gaming, local hardware will likely still provide the most responsive experience.

b) Offline Play: Cloud gaming needs a constant internet connection, which may not be available in all locations. In remote places, or if your internet link is unreliable, a powerful gaming laptop will still be necessary for offline play. Future gaming laptops will need to support both cloud gaming and local gaming, allowing versatility for gamers who want the best of both worlds.

c) VR and Esports: For immersive experiences such as VR gaming or high-level esports, local hardware will still play a critical part. Even with improvements in cloud gaming, VR experiences require low latency and powerful processing, which is difficult to achieve via streaming. Similarly, expert esports players rely on high-performance systems to ensure the lowest possible latency and the best frame rates.

Why It's Important: While cloud gaming will provide more flexibility and lower hardware requirements for casual gaming, high-performance gaming laptops will still be important for competitive gaming, VR, and offline play.

In conclusion, the future of gaming laptops is incredibly exciting, with advancements in AI, 5G connectivity, cloud gaming, and laptop design all working together to push the limits of what is possible in portable gaming. Gaming laptops will continue to change, offering more powerful systems that are also lighter, thinner, and more versatile.

At the same time, cloud gaming will offer new possibilities for casual gamers, allowing them to play high-end games without the need for expensive hardware. As the technology progresses, gaming laptops will become a cornerstone of the gaming experience, evolving to meet the demands of modern gamers.

Conclusion

Wrapping Up and Staying Informed

As we come to the end of this comprehensive manual on gaming laptops, it's important to take a moment to reflect on the key takeaways. Choosing the right gaming laptop involves evaluating a variety of factors, from performance and price to design and compatibility. Whether you're a casual gamer, an esports enthusiast, or someone looking to push the limits with VR gaming, there's a gaming laptop for you in 2024. By carefully considering the features, performance specs, and future trends outlined in this guide, you can make an informed choice that meets your needs and improves your gaming experience.

Wrapping Up: Making Your Final Decision
By now, you should have a clear idea of what to look for in a gaming laptop, and you've seen the wide array of options available based on your budget, gaming style, and preferred features. But when it comes time

to make your final choice, here are some steps to help you choose:

1. Assess Your Needs:

Think about what type of games you plan to play and the results you expect. Casual gamers who play lighter titles like Minecraft or Fortnite may find budget or mid-range laptops more than suitable. On the other hand, if you're an esports player or someone who enjoys visually demanding AAA titles, investing in a high-end gaming laptop with top-tier components like an RTX 3080 or RTX 4090 might be the right choice.

2. Set a Budget:

It's important to set a clear budget before shopping. Gaming computers can range from under $800 for budget models to over $2,000 for high-end machines. Knowing your budget will help narrow down your choices and prevent you from overspending on things you don't need.

3. Prioritize Key Features:

Consider which features mean most to you. Do you favor display quality for immersive graphics, or do you need a high refresh rate for esports? Is portability a worry for gaming on the go, or is power and performance more important for gaming sessions at home? Make sure to choose a laptop that aligns with your individual preferences.

4. Don't Forget About the Extras:

Gaming laptops are often more than just gaming tools. Look for additional features like long battery life, customizable RGB lighting, and a high-quality keyboard that improve your overall experience. These extras can make a major difference in comfort and enjoyment.

5. Check Reviews and User Feedback:

Before making a final buy, check user reviews, expert opinions, and benchmark tests for the specific model you're interested in. Seeing how others have experienced the laptop in real-world situations will give you insight into potential issues or advantages that you may not have considered.

How to Stay Informed and Keep Your Gaming Setup Current

The world of gaming laptops is constantly evolving, with new hardware, software, and features launched each year. To stay ahead of the curve and ensure your gaming setting remains current, here are some tips:

1. Follow Industry News:

Stay updated about the latest trends in gaming laptops by following trusted tech websites, online forums, and social media channels dedicated to gaming hardware. Websites like Anand Tech, Tom's Hardware, and PC Gamer regularly post news, reviews, and scores on the newest models and technologies. Following these sites will help you stay updated on the latest releases and developments in the gaming laptop world.

2. Participate in Gaming Communities:

Online communities, including subreddits like r/gaming laptops and r/pc master race, provide useful feedback from fellow gamers who are passionate about gaming hardware. By joining these communities, you can exchange insights, ask for help, and get real-time information on the performance of particular gaming laptops.

3. Upgrade When Necessary:

As gaming technology improves, laptops may become outdated more quickly. To keep your laptop current, consider upgrading components such as RAM or storage (if possible), or invest in peripherals like a new gaming mouse or external monitor to improve your setup. This can give your system a performance boost without needing to replace the full laptop.

4. Cloud Gaming as a Supplement:

While you may still need a high-performance laptop for local gaming, the rise of cloud gaming can help you stay linked to new titles without constantly upgrading your laptop. Services like NVIDIA GeForce Now, Xbox Cloud Gaming, and Amazon Luna are great ways to play high-quality games on a lower-spec machine. Staying involved with cloud gaming platforms ensures that you can access the latest games without requiring the latest hardware.

5. Monitor Your Laptop's Health:

Regular maintenance of your game laptop will extend its lifespan and keep it running at its best. Clean the vents, update drivers, monitor speed through software like HW Monitor or MSI Afterburner, and keep your system free from unnecessary software. These simple practices will ensure that your laptop stays efficient and free of issues that can impact gaming performance.

6. Consider Your Next Upgrade:

If you find that your laptop struggles to run new games at high settings, it might be time to consider an upgrade. The hardware landscape moves quickly, and if you want to stay ahead in competitive gaming or ensure a smooth experience with the latest AAA games, upgrading to a new model or even an entirely new setup might be necessary.

Final Thoughts

Choosing the right gaming laptop is an exciting and important choice. Whether you're a casual gamer on a budget or a competitive player wanting high-end performance, there's a laptop out there for you. Keep in mind that the gaming laptop market is constantly changing, and staying informed about the latest trends and technological advancements will help you make smarter decisions when it comes time to upgrade.

By carefully considering your gaming needs, budget, and future-proofing choices, you can find a laptop that will serve you well for years to come. Don't forget to keep your gaming setup current by staying informed, upgrading components when possible, and taking advantage of cloud gaming platforms for freedom.

Happy gaming, and may your gaming laptop always work at its best!

Appendix

This appendix offers extra resources to help you navigate the world of gaming laptops. Whether you're new to gaming laptops or an experienced enthusiast, understanding key terms, exploring valuable online communities, and knowing which brands are worth considering can greatly improve your overall gaming experience.

Glossary of Gaming Laptop Terms

1. CPU (Central Processing Unit):

Often referred to as the "brain" of the laptop, the CPU handles the instructions and task that the system performs. In gaming laptops, a powerful CPU is important for smooth gameplay, especially in CPU-intensive titles.

2. GPU (Graphics Processing Unit):

The GPU is responsible for creating graphics, textures, and animations in games. It plays a significant part in how games look and perform. High-end GPUs, like the NVIDIA GeForce RTX series, are critical for running modern AAA games at high settings.

3. RAM (Random Access Memory):

RAM stores temporary data and instructions that are constantly used by the CPU. More RAM allows for better multitasking and faster loading times in games. Gaming laptops usually come with 8GB to 32GB of RAM, depending on the model.

4. SSD (Solid-State Drive):

An SSD is a type of storage device that offers faster read and write speeds compared to standard HDDs (Hard Disk Drives). SSDs dramatically improve loading times in games and the general speed of the system.

5. Refresh Rate:

The refresh rate refers to how many times per second the display refreshes the picture on the screen. Measured in Hz, a higher refresh rate (e.g., 144Hz, 240Hz) results in smoother visuals, especially in fast-paced games where high responsiveness is important.

6. Thermal Throttling:

Thermal throttling happens when a laptop's internal components, especially the CPU and GPU, overheat and automatically reduce their performance to prevent damage. Good cooling systems help prevent thermal throttling, ensuring sustained performance during long game sessions.

7. RGB Lighting:

RGB lighting refers to customizable lighting effects that are often found on game keyboards, mice, and laptop chassis. Many gaming laptops offer RGB options, allowing you to personalize the lighting based on your tastes or sync it with gameplay.

8. FPS (Frames Per Second):

FPS refers to how many frames the laptop can display per second. Higher FPS (e.g., 60 FPS, 120 FPS, 144 FPS) results in smoother and more responsive gameplay, which is important for competitive gaming.

9. Ray Tracing:

Ray tracing is an advanced graphics rendering method that simulates how light behaves in real life. It produces more realistic lighting, shadows, and reflections in games. It's a feature supported by NVIDIA's RTX line GPUs.

10. G-Sync / FreeSync:

G-Sync (by NVIDIA) and FreeSync (by AMD) are technologies that synchronize the refresh rate of the monitor with the GPU's frame rate to eliminate screen tearing and stuttering during gameplay, giving a smoother visual experience.

Additional Resources: Websites, Forums, and Communities

Staying informed about the latest trends, hardware, and troubleshooting tips is important for every gaming laptop owner. Here are some key websites, forums, and communities that can provide useful insights and information:

1. Tom's Hardware Website:

https://www.tomshardware.com
A top resource for hardware reviews, buying guides, and troubleshooting tips. Tom's Hardware covers everything from gaming laptops to desktop PCs and offers in-depth technical content.

2. PC Gamer Website:

https://www.pcgamer.com

A popular gaming site giving reviews, news, and guides on all things gaming, including laptops, gaming PCs, and peripherals. Their gaming laptop reviews are thorough and detailed.

3. AnandTech Website:

https://www.anandtech.com

Known for its technical reviews and benchmarks, AnandTech is a great resource for anyone interested in performance research of gaming laptops and components.

4. Reddit - r/gaminglaptops Forum:

https://www.reddit.com/r/gaminglaptops

A subreddit dedicated to gaming laptops where users share reviews, experiences, and tips. It's a great place to ask questions, get recommendations, and discuss all things connected to gaming laptops.

5. Linus Tech Tips Forum Forum:

https://linustechtips.com

A popular tech group giving a vast range of discussions on gaming laptops, hardware upgrades, and troubleshooting. The forum is very busy, and you can find help from both tech enthusiasts and professionals.

6. NotebookCheck Website:

https://www.notebookcheck.net

A useful resource for gaming laptop reviews, benchmarks, and comparisons. NotebookCheck offers detailed performance tests, helping you make informed choices when purchasing gaming laptops.

7. Overclock.net Forum: https:

//www.overclock.net

Overclock.net is a great place for enthusiasts who want to push the edges of their hardware. You can find tips for overclocking gaming laptops, as well as reviews and suggestions.

Recommended Gaming Laptop Brands

When choosing a gaming laptop, brand reputation plays a crucial part in ensuring quality, performance, and customer support. Here are some of the best gaming laptop brands known for providing top-tier gaming experiences:

1. Alienware (by Dell)

Known for its premium game laptops with exceptional performance and bold designs, Alienware offers powerful systems with excellent cooling, top-tier GPUs, and advanced displays. Alienware laptops are a top choice for serious gamers and those looking for high-end gaming machines. Popular Models: Alienware x17, Alienware m15

2. Razer

Razer is famous for its sleek, stylish gaming laptops that offer high performance in a portable form. Known for its RGB lights and premium build quality, Razer's laptops are favored by gamers who want both power and style.

Popular Models: Razer Blade 15, Razer Blade Stealth

3. ASUS ROG (Republic of Gamers)

ASUS ROG is one of the most recognized names in the gaming laptop world, offering a wide range of laptops with high-end specs, better cooling, and customizable features. ASUS ROG laptops are often equipped with the latest NVIDIA RTX GPUs and Intel or AMD Ryzen CPUs.

Popular Models: ASUS ROG Strix G15, ASUS ROG Zephyrus G14

4. MSI

MSI is known for making gaming laptops that provide excellent performance at competitive prices. MSI laptops are designed to handle intensive gaming tasks and are often equipped with high refresh rate displays and RTX GPUs.

Popular Models: MSI GE76 Raider, MSI GS66 Stealth

5. HP Omen

HP Omen is HP's flagship game line, known for its solid build quality, powerful components, and great value for money. HP Omen laptops often feature RTX graphics and high refresh rate screens, catering to players who want premium performance without the premium price tag.

Popular Models: HP Omen 15, HP Omen 17

6. Lenovo Legion

Lenovo Legion laptops are famous for their excellent build quality, solid gaming performance, and user-friendly design. The Legion line combines high-end components with affordability, making them an excellent choice for gamers on a budget who don't want to compromise on performance.

Popular Models: Lenovo Legion 5, Lenovo Legion 7i

7. Gigabyte AORUS

Gigabyte AORUS offers high-performance laptops aimed at gamers and content makers who need the best in speed, graphics, and multitasking. With excellent build quality, RTX GPUs, and cutting-edge cooling systems, AORUS laptops are intended for enthusiasts.

Popular Models: AORUS 15G, AORUS 17G